# The UK Wine Industry

## Profiles of the leading 300 companies

John D Blackburn

Editor

First Edition

Spring 2019

ISBN-13: 978-1-912736-14-0

ISBN-10: 1-912736-14-4

All rights reserved. No part of this publication may be reproduced, distributed, or transmitted in any form or by any means, including photocopying, recording, or other electronic or mechanical methods, without our prior written permission, except in the case of brief quotations embodied in critical reviews and certain other non-commercial uses permitted by copyright law. For permission requests, please write to us.

Copyright © 2019 Dellam Publishing Limited

Printed in 8pt Nimbus Sans L

Designed by URW++ Design and Development GmbH

Dellam Publishing Limited

2 Heath Drive, Sutton, Surrey, SM2 5RP

Fax: 020 8770 7478    email: enquiries@dellam.com

SAN: 0177881    EAN/GLN: 5030670177882

## Table of Contents

1 Acknowledgements .......................................................... iv

2 Introduction .................................................................. v

3 Total Assets League Table ................................................. 1
- As a measure of size, total assets is preferable to turnover which is influenced by profit margins and whether companies are capital or labour intensive.

4 Age of Companies ........................................................... 5
- Each company is ranked by its date of incorporation. Newcomers are defined as those registered since 2017.

5 Geographic Distribution .................................................... 9
- Each company is classed by county.

6 Company Profiles ........................................................... 13
- Full company name, date incorporated, net worth, total assets, registered office, activities, shareholders and parent company, directors (with date of birth, nationality and occupation) and number of employees (if available).

7 Index of Directorships ..................................................... 33
- Alphabetical list of directors showing their directorships. If several directors have identical names then their date of birth is shown.

8 Standard Industrial Classification ....................................... 41
- These codes are used to classify businesses by the type of economic activity in which they are engaged.

9 *finis* ........................................................................ 44

## Acknowledgements

This is a long and detailed publication containing thousands of facts and figures. It is only to be expected, despite continuous and repeated editing and checking, that errors may occur. In such cases, once we are aware of any, we publish a correction on our website.

**Readers are encouraged to check regularly at www.dellam.com/books for any corrections and updates.**

Although we take extreme care to ensure accuracy and being up-to-date, we cannot accept responsibility for any errors or omissions.

Contains public sector information licensed under Open Government Licence v3.0. from The Charity Commission (England and Wales) and The Charity Commission for Northern Ireland. © Crown Copyright and database right (2018).

Contains information from the Scottish Charity Register supplied by the Office of the Scottish Charity Regulator and licensed under the Open Government Licence v.2.0. © Crown Copyright and database right (2018).

Contains OS data © Crown copyright and database right (2018)

Contains Royal Mail data © Royal Mail copyright and database right (2018)

Contains National Statistics data © Crown copyright and database right (2018)

Contains Office for National Statistics © Crown copyright and database right (2018)

Maps based on those produced by the Office for National Statistics Geography GIS & Mapping Unit (2012 and 2018).

Contains HM Land Registry data © Crown copyright and database right (2018).

Contains Parliamentary information licensed under the Open Parliament Licence v3.0.

House of Commons Library Briefing Papers licensed under the Open Parliament Licence v3.0.

Contains Food Standards Agency data © Crown copyright and database right (2018).

Contains Eurostat data, 1995-2018, copyright European Commission by the Decision of 12 December 2011.

Maps based on produced by ONS Geography GIS & Mapping Unit.

Contains Companies House data supplied under section 47 and 50 of the Copyright, Designs and Patents Act 1988 and Schedule 1 of the Database Regulations (SI 1997/3032).

We appreciate your interest in our publications, and your comments and suggestions are always welcome. Please contact us at enquiries@dellam.com.

# Introduction

This study looks at all companies registered in the United Kingdom where they identify themselves as wine makers.

This study includes companies that are dormant or non-trading some of which might be latent while others may operate under their owners' names but are incorporated to protect the business name. In addition, all newly incorporated companies are included. The study will exclude those companies that do not specifically identify themselves as wine makers.

The aim of this study is to provide an overview of the key movers and shakers in the UK wine sector. Only key data has been isolated, particularly the company's net worth and total assets, but also its full name, date incorporated, registered office, other activities, shareholders, directors (with date of birth, occupation and nationality) and number of employees.

Two indicators of size are used: net worth and total assets. These are preferable to turnover which is influenced by profit margins and whether the companies are capital or labour intensive.

In the years 2016, 2017 and 2018, new company incorporations in the wine sector were 27, 33 and 64 respectively.

The productive area for the 2015 harvest was estimated to be approximately 1,839 hectares. The largest area under cultivation was Kent (344 hectares) followed by West Sussex (296), Hampshire (235), East Sussex (231) Surrey (132) and Essex (119). There are now almost 40 hectares of vines planted in Wales.

The main vine varieties grown in the UK are Chardonnay (approx 518 hectares) and Pinot Noir (approx 483 hectares). The other classic sparkling varieties account for 194 hectares. The classic sparkling wines make up over 60% of the planted area within the UK.

Just over 38,000 hectolitres of wine were produced in 2015. The 2014 harvest was the largest ever with 48,267 hectolitres of wine being produced.

There were 523 registered vineyards and 133 wineries in 2017.

United Kingdom Vineyards Association (UKVA) and English Wine Producers (EWP) merged in 2017 to form Wines of Great Britain (WineGB), the new national organisation for grape growers and winemakers. WineGB reported as follows: 2,500 hectares under vine, with around 700 vineyards (not all commercial); 5.9 million bottles produced in 2017; sales grew by 31% between 2015 and 2017 and approx 2,100 full-time employees and wines sales are £10.9 billion.

More than 11,000 pubs have closed in the UK in the last decade, a fall of almost a quarter (23%). The number of UK pubs has fallen from around 50,000 in 2008 to some 39,000 in 2018. Although many pubs have closed, the total turnover of pubs and bars has held up, remaining flat since 2008, adjusting for inflation. Around 70% of workers in pubs and bars are paid less than the Living Wage Foundation's living wage.

Standard cataloguing guidelines for company names in the profile section have been used, but there will be occurrences when the name may not be strictly alphabetical. A certain licence was adopted where it was felt that strictly alphabetical could lead to improper cataloguing. Some company names have been shortened in the league tables for aesthetic reasons.

John D Blackburn
Editor

*This page is intentionally left blank*

# Total Assets League Table

| Company | Value | Company | Value |
|---|---|---|---|
| Accolade Wines Limited | £333,712,000 | Woodchester Valley Winery Limited | £1,237,146 |
| Treasury Wine Estates EMEA Limited | £205,760,000 | Digby Wine Ltd | £1,219,494 |
| Treasury Wine Estates UK Brands Limited | £92,878,672 | Digby Fine English Ltd | £1,218,131 |
| FBL Holdings Limited | £75,101,000 | Vergecosse Limited | £1,211,981 |
| TWE Finance (UK) Limited | £60,580,812 | Duncairn Wines Limited | £1,188,302 |
| Silva and Cosens Limited | £47,200,000 | Andreas Wine Trading Ltd | £1,158,806 |
| Chapel Down Group PLC | £39,469,820 | The Global Winery Limited | £1,034,675 |
| Continental Wine & Food Limited | £37,602,080 | Upperton Vineyards Limited | £983,512 |
| Cellarmaster Wines Holdings (UK) Limited | £29,715,000 | Santa Rita Europe Limited | £980,211 |
| Broadland Wineries Limited | £24,202,070 | South East Wineries Limited | £951,756 |
| Nyetimber Limited | £19,428,544 | Gowine Limited | £878,195 |
| Gusbourne PLC | £17,466,000 | Lindisfarne Limited | £811,398 |
| World Wine Investors UK Limited | £16,683,761 | Deviock Wine Company Limited | £676,696 |
| Gusbourne Estate Limited | £16,207,621 | Albourne Winery Limited | £660,981 |
| Hattingley Valley Wines Limited | £10,070,034 | Giffords Hall Vineyard Limited | £646,085 |
| English Wines PLC | £9,769,827 | Bluebell Vineyard Estates Limited | £627,579 |
| Robert Roberts (NI) Limited | £8,779,544 | Carr Taylor Wines Limited | £624,786 |
| Ridgeview Estate Winery Limited | £6,271,342 | Stanlake Park Company Limited | £619,355 |
| Hambledon Vineyard PLC | £5,263,902 | Court Garden Limited | £576,503 |
| Hambledon Wineries Limited | £5,236,812 | London Cru Ltd | £556,837 |
| Kingscote Investments Limited | £4,822,644 | Stopham Vineyard Ltd | £536,835 |
| Greyfriars Vineyard Limited | £4,632,057 | Yorkshire Heart Limited | £508,433 |
| Evremond Estate Limited | £4,366,007 | Langham Wine Limited | £503,274 |
| Spirits Development & Management Company (SDMC) | £3,439,762 | Nutbourne Vineyards Limited | £479,222 |
| Bolney Wine Estate Ltd | £3,276,272 | Shawsgate Limited | £433,487 |
| The Stonor Valley Winery Limited | £3,215,818 | Henners Limited | £338,409 |
| Three Choirs Vineyards Limited | £2,999,865 | Enborne Vineyards Limited | £338,224 |
| Camel Valley Limited | £2,840,769 | Green Ridge Wines Ltd | £332,452 |
| Simpsons Wine Estate Limited | £2,802,821 | Casa Vizzini Ltd | £330,300 |
| Southern England Wines (UK) Ltd | £2,754,968 | Plummerden Estates Limited | £324,842 |
| Rudd Farms Limited | £2,364,268 | Plummerden Lane Vineyards Limited | £323,087 |
| Direct Wine Factory Ltd | £2,174,676 | Dedham Vale Vineyard Limited | £302,745 |
| St Emilion Holdings Limited | £2,159,654 | Somerby Vineyards Limited | £291,551 |
| Pinglestone Estate Limited | £2,147,771 | G.I.V. UK Ltd | £281,217 |
| Westwell Wine Estates Ltd | £2,122,114 | Maud Heath Wine Trading Limited | £264,597 |
| Michel Couvreur (Scotch Whiskies) Limited | £2,077,092 | Poulton Hill Estate Limited | £237,358 |
| Coates and Seely Limited | £1,891,802 | Herbert Hall Wines Limited | £221,504 |
| Skinnybrands Ltd | £1,702,059 | Danebury Vineyards Limited | £205,385 |
| The Wine Fusion Limited | £1,592,013 | Flint & Vine Limited | £193,259 |
| Danbury Wine Estate Limited | £1,584,899 | Globus Wines (UK) Ltd | £191,132 |
| Chalk House Vineyard Limited | £1,493,054 | Creative Wine Making Limited | £189,619 |
| Sharpham Partnership Limited | £1,427,812 | Tillingham Wines Limited | £189,541 |
| Harrow & Hope Limited | £1,254,141 | Pharos AC Ltd. | £188,151 |

| Company | Amount | Company | Amount |
|---|---|---|---|
| Chiltern Valley Liqueur Producers, Brewers & Vintners | £185,379 | Kingscote Winery Ltd | £32,213 |
| Weinhouse Limited | £183,224 | Amber Valley Wines Ltd | £25,507 |
| Lines Brew Co Ltd | £167,946 | Bibelot Wine Ltd | £24,452 |
| Black Dog Hill Estates Ltd | £163,061 | Viniage Wines Limited | £24,020 |
| General Bilimoria Wines Limited | £152,257 | Bath Sparkling Wine Company Ltd | £23,735 |
| Rosemary Vineyard Ltd. | £143,479 | Strawberry Bank Liqueurs Limited | £23,585 |
| Sugrue Pierre Limited | £130,505 | Welland Valley Vineyard Ltd | £22,171 |
| The Boutique Cellar Limited | £128,656 | Walton Brook Vineyard Limited | £20,524 |
| Somborne Valley Vineyard Limited | £125,200 | The Derbyshire Winery Limited | £20,023 |
| Mereworth Wines Limited | £123,638 | Premia Wines Ltd. | £19,429 |
| Global Wine Solutions Limited | £120,305 | Great Canney Vineyards Limited | £17,967 |
| The Verrillo Partnership Limited | £117,415 | Polmassick Vineyard Limited | £16,259 |
| Carter's Vineyards Ltd | £106,499 | Our Fathers Wines Ltd | £14,333 |
| Fleur Fields Limited | £99,858 | The Vineyard Dynamics Co. Limited | £12,988 |
| Fair Services Limited | £96,575 | Exe Valley Wines Limited | £12,691 |
| Urban Initiatives Limited | £89,136 | K1 Beer PLC | £12,046 |
| A'Beckett's Vineyard Limited | £87,719 | Winebar Pouch Company Ltd | £11,996 |
| UK Wine Services Limited | £84,626 | Simpsons Wine Imports Limited | £11,098 |
| Furleigh Estate (Winery) Ltd | £71,784 | Rockfield Wines Limited | £10,713 |
| Piersons Spirit of Wine Consulting Ltd | £68,262 | Witham Wines Limited | £10,691 |
| Fiamma & Ivo Limited | £61,430 | Rose Wine Ltd. | £6,958 |
| Wroxeter Roman Vineyard Ltd | £59,859 | Dryhill Wine Ltd | £5,521 |
| Torview Wines Limited | £51,298 | Creoda's Hill Ltd | £5,509 |
| Avanti Wines Ltd | £50,146 | Conradie-Penhill Wines UK Ltd. | £4,911 |
| Castlewood Vineyards Ltd | £49,893 | Guinexport Trade and Services Limited | £1,872 |
| Casa Divertente Limited | £48,737 | De Noble Vines Limited | £1,350 |
| Dinton Wines Limited | £44,854 | South East Vineyards Association Ltd | £1,201 |
| D'Urberville Vineyard Limited | £42,492 | Bsixtwelve Limited | £997 |
| Wolf Oak Limited | £42,329 | Dorchester Vineyard Limited | £100 |
| Atkinson Wines Ltd | £41,862 | Sant' Elia Limited | £100 |
| Rothley Wine Limited | £41,712 | Acloque Capital Limited | £100 |
| Villa Maria New Zealand Wineries (UK) Limited | £40,024 | Crundale Wines Limited | £100 |
| Gwinllan Conwy Ltd | £38,436 | Realsa Wines Import & Export Ltd | £58 |
| Strawberry Hill Vineyard Limited | £37,428 | Brightday Enterprises Limited | £4 |
| Binfield Vineyard Limited | £34,308 | Montgomery Vineyard Limited | £1 |
| Amwell Springs Brewery Company Limited | £33,156 | Celebrated Wines Limited | £1 |

*This page is intentionally left blank*

# Age of Companies

**1910-1919**
Accolade Wines Limited
Silva and Cosens Limited

**1960-1969**
Broadland Wineries Limited
Cellarmaster Wines Holdings (UK) Ltd
Continental Wine & Food Ltd
Duncairn Wines Limited

**1970-1979**
Court Garden Limited
Lindisfarne Limited
Stangro Limited
Stanlake Park Co Ltd

**1980-1989** [5]
Bluebell Vineyard Estates Ltd
Michel Couvreur (Scotch Whiskies)
Three Choirs Vineyards Limited
Treasury Wine Estates EMEA Ltd
Welland Valley Vineyard Ltd

**1990-1994** [5]
Beringer Blass Wine Estates Ltd
Danebury Vineyards Limited
New Zealand Wine Club Limited
Sharpham Partnership Limited
Southcorp Wines Europe Limited

**1995**
Ridgeview Estate Winery Ltd

**1997**
G.I.V. UK Ltd
Gowine Limited

**1998**
Fair Services Limited

**1999**
James Herrick Wines Limited
Victor Lanson Limited
Lanson UK Limited
Shawsgate Limited

**2000**
A'Beckett's Vineyard Limited
Carr Taylor Wines Limited
English Wines PLC
United Manufacturing Europe Ltd

**2001**
Binfield Vineyard Limited
Camel Valley Limited
Ridgeview Winery Contracts Ltd
Somborne Valley Vineyard Ltd

**2002** [10]
Bibelot Wine Ltd
Brightday Enterprises Limited
Chapel Down Group PLC
Exe Valley Wines Limited
Fleur Fields Limited
Global Winery Limited
Robert Roberts (NI) Limited
Simpsons Wine Imports Limited
Strawberry Bank Liqueurs Ltd
Sutter Home Winery Limited

**2003** [5]
Bolney Wine Estate Ltd
Harrow & Hope Limited
Heartland Wines Europe Limited
Ludlow Vineyard Limited
Santa Rita Europe Limited

**2004**
Marmoreccia Limited

**2005**
La Remonta Limited
Nutbourne Vineyards Limited
Nyetimber Limited

**2006**
Henners Limited
Somerby Vineyards Limited
Sussex Vineyards Limited
Vergecosse Limited

**2007** [5]
De Noble Vines Limited
Deviock Wine Co Ltd
Herbert Hall Wines Limited
Maud Heath Wine Trading Ltd
St Emilion Holdings Limited

**2008**
Coates and Seely Limited
FBL Holdings Limited
Stopham Vineyard Ltd
Wine Fusion Limited

**2009** [10]
Enjoy Wine Ltd
Ergene Holding (UK) Ltd.
General Bilimoria Wines Ltd
Globus Wines (UK) Ltd
Hambledon Wineries Limited
Rose Wine Ltd.
Sloegasm Limited
Torview Wines Limited
Vineyard Dynamics Co. Limited
Wine Fusion Innovations Ltd

**July-December 2010** [6]
Albourne Winery Limited
Derbyshire Winery Limited
Greyfriars Vineyard Limited
Hambledon Vineyard PLC
Hattingley Valley Wines Ltd
Strawberry Hill Vineyard Ltd

**January-June 2011** [9]
Amber Valley Wines Ltd
Chapel Down Group Ltd
Furleigh Estate (Winery) Ltd
Gusbourne Estate Limited
Hampshire Wines Limited
TWE Finance (UK) Limited
Treasury Wine Estates UK Brands Ltd
Wroxeter Roman Vineyard Ltd
Yorkshire Heart Limited

**July-December 2011** [5]
Enborne Vineyards Limited
Kingscote Winery Ltd
Langham Wine Limited
Poulton Hill Estate Limited
Rosemary Vineyard Ltd.

**January-March 2012**
Giffords Hall Vineyard Limited

**April-June 2012**
Boutique Cellar Limited
Carter's Vineyards Ltd
Digby Fine English Ltd
Digby Wine Ltd

**July-September 2012** [5]
Boars Hill Farm Limited
Gusbourne PLC
K1 Beer PLC
London Cru Ltd
World Wine Investors UK Ltd

**October-December 2012** [6]
Chalk House Vineyard Limited
Danbury Wine Estate Limited
Dedham Vale Vineyard Limited
Dorchester Vineyard Limited
South East Vineyards Association Ltd
Stonor Valley Winery Limited

**January-March 2013**
Blaxsta UK Limited
Bolney Vineyards Ltd
Qualpro Greece Ltd.
Sugrue Pierre Limited

**April-June 2013** [5]
Direct Wine Factory Ltd
Eco Vino Limited
Fiamma & Ivo Limited
Polmassick Vineyard Limited
Wolf Oak Limited

**July-September 2013**
Dinton Wines Limited
Laurel Vines, Vineyard & Winery Ltd
Plummerden Lane Vineyards Ltd
Viniage Wines Limited

**October-December 2013** [7]
Avanti Wines Ltd
Breaky Bottom Ltd
Plummerden Estates Limited
Sant' Elia Limited
Simpsons Wine Estate Limited
Spirits Development & Management Company (SDMC)
Winebar Pouch Co Ltd

**January-March 2014** [6]
Creative Wine Making Limited
Mayfield Vineyards Ltd
Our Fathers Wines Ltd
Piersons Spirit of Wine Consulting Ltd
Rothley Wine Limited
Weinhouse Limited

**April-June 2014**
Black Dog Hill Estates Ltd
Premia Wines Ltd.

# The UK Wine Industry

**July-September 2014**
Green Ridge Wines Ltd
Montgomery Vineyard Limited
Walton Brook Vineyard Limited

**October-December 2014**
Chiltern Valley Liqueur Producers, Brewers & Vintners
Guinexport Trade and Services Ltd
Realsa Wines Import & Export Ltd
Woodchester Valley Winery Ltd

**March 2015**
Andreas Wine Trading Ltd
Bath Sparkling Wine Co Ltd
Conradie-Penhill Wines UK Ltd.

**April 2015**
Evremond Estate Limited

**May 2015**
Pharos AC Ltd.

**June 2015**
Flint & Vine Limited
Port O' Bristol Ltd

**July 2015**
Karmely Limited
Villa Maria New Zealand Wineries (UK)

**September 2015**
Skinnybrands Ltd

**October 2015**
Acloque Capital Limited

**November 2015**
Rudd Farms Limited

**January 2016**
San Gregorio UK Limited

**February 2016**
Castlewood Vineyards Ltd
Creoda's Hill Ltd
Kingwood Estate Limited
Rockfield Wines Limited

**March 2016** [6]
Gwinllan Conwy Ltd
Mereworth Wines Limited
Off The Line Limited
Southern England Wines (UK) Ltd
Upperton Vineyards Limited
Vine Revival UK Limited

**April 2016**
Beacon Down Vineyard Ltd
Casa Vizzini Ltd
Dryhill Wine Ltd
Witham Wines Limited

**May 2016**
Lines Brew Co Ltd
Mastropasqua & Brothers Ltd.

**June 2016**
Forgeron Dubois Limited
Urban Initiatives Limited

**July 2016**
Harmony Vineyard Ltd.

**September 2016**
Celebrated Wines Limited
T & P Weinbau

**October 2016**
Global Wine Solutions Limited

**November 2016**
D'Urberville Vineyard Limited
UK Wine Services Limited

**December 2016**
Great Canney Vineyards Limited
Pinglestone Estate Limited

**January 2017**
Barramundi Wines Ltd
Casa Divertente Limited

**February 2017**
Bsixtwelve Limited
Kingscote Investments Limited
Tillingham Wines Limited

**March 2017**
Atkinson Wines Ltd
Verrillo Partnership Limited

**April 2017**
Enlightened Entrepreneur Ltd
Nyetimber (International Operations)
Weyborne Limited

**May 2017**
Swift Half Collective Ltd

**June 2017**
Davenport Vineyards Limited
Westwell Wine Estates Ltd
Wines of Douro Limited

**July 2017**
Amwell Springs Brewery Co Ltd
Busi-Jacobsohn Wine Estate Ltd
Caxdon Premier Limited
Crundale Wines Limited

**August 2017**
Arctic Wine Limited
Vesteraalen Vinproduksjon Ltd

**September 2017**
Laneberg Wine Ltd
Leskaroon Falls Wine Estate Ltd
South East Wineries Limited

**October 2017** [5]
Ghenos Vineyard Estates Ltd
Little Horse Wines Limited
Luxbev Limited
Silverton Wines Ltd
Tinston Wines & Ciders Limited

**November 2017**
Bahlina Ltd
Oastbrook Estates Limited

**December 2017**
Somm in the Must Ltd
Taylor Family Wines Ltd.
Too Far North Wine Co Ltd

**January 2018**
Brighton and Hove Wine Co Ltd
Chinese Baijiu Association Ltd
Grape Fun Limited
Itasca Wines Limited

**February 2018** [5]
Amor Food and Beverages Holdings Ltd
Evremond Vineyards Limited
Kidmore Vineyard Ltd
Kingsthorne Limited
Vinus Wine Ltd

**March 2018**
AB Vaults Group Limited
Luminati Wine Limited
Alistair McCoist & Jeff East (Vintners)
Noahs Estate Ltd

**April 2018**
Alko Vintages UK Ltd
Amont Products Limited
Ben Flower Limited
Nuclearbest Ltd

**May 2018** [9]
B & F Enterprise UK Ltd
BF Wines UK Ltd
Embev Ltd
Engstrom Group Ltd
Magnus Wines Ltd
Mersea Island Brewery & Vineyard Ltd
Penselwood Partnership Ltd
Skyblossom Ltd
Universal Robo Innovations Ltd

**June 2018**
Alcohol Beverages Co Ltd
Audiozine Ltd
Cool Brew Dept Ltd
Uponcellar Ltd

**July 2018** [9]
Bigmite Ltd
Braidclift Ltd
Fruito Beverages (Africa) Ltd
Maskstice Ltd
Mosrowes Ltd
Nimblusher Ltd
Podere Delle Rune Ltd
Pure Winery Limited
River Valley Vineyards Limited

**August 2018**
Lakemercy Ltd
Rebel Pi Limited
Ross Earl Wine Co., Ltd.
Sapphiremimic Ltd

**September 2018** [6]
Aeropica Ltd
Devine Distillates Group (Manufacturing)
Heron Ventures Ltd
Press Shed Wines Limited
Sibling Winery Limited
Tewaina Ltd

**October 2018** [5]
Able G Limited

Green Evolution Products Ltd
Medland Manor Vineyard Ltd.
Oui Vino Limited
Selectia Wine Ltd

**November 2018** [7]
Bathinmaestro Ltd
Cotswold Wine Estate Ltd
Defined Wine Ltd
Dropmore Vineyard Ltd
Polgoon Vineyard Ltd
Schoenlaub Limited
Winehood Ltd

**December 2018**
Bach & Co Solution Limited
Clandestine Distillery Limited
Drinktonics Limited

**January 2019** [9]
B & M Wines Ltd
Daavan Two Limited
Flower Miners Limited
Gavioli Ltd
Green Evolution Production Ltd
KMSFish One Limited
Sharpham Wine Limited
Tremayne Food and Drink Ltd
Vitosha Wine Ltd

**February 2019**
Highbrook Wine Estate Limited
Oeno Group Ltd
Sticle Vineyard Ltd
Wild Life Botanicals Ltd

# Geographic Distribution by County

**Co Antrim**
Duncairn Wines Limited
Robert Roberts (NI) Limited

**Aberdeenshire**
Michel Couvreur (Scotch Whiskies)

**Lanarkshire**
Alistair McCoist & Jeff East (Vintners)
Rose Wine Ltd.
Uponcellar Ltd

**Berkshire** [10]
Amor Food and Beverages Holdings Ltd
Binfield Vineyard Limited
Enborne Vineyards Limited
Evremond Estate Limited
Evremond Vineyards Limited
Kidmore Vineyard Ltd
Kingwood Estate Limited
Premia Wines Ltd.
Stanlake Park Co Ltd
Villa Maria New Zealand Wineries (UK)

**Buckinghamshire**
Boars Hill Farm Limited
Dinton Wines Limited
Harrow & Hope Limited

**Cambridgeshire**
Guinexport Trade and Services Ltd

**Carmarthenshire**
Sticle Vineyard Ltd

**Cheshire**
Andreas Wine Trading Ltd
Henners Limited
KMSFish One Limited
Luminati Wine Limited

**Clwyd**
Gwinllan Conwy Ltd

**Co Derry**
Too Far North Wine Co Ltd

**Co Durham**
Wine Fusion Limited

**Cornwall** [8]
Camel Valley Limited
Deviock Wine Co Ltd
Drinktonics Limited
Flower Miners Limited
Oui Vino Limited
Polgoon Vineyard Ltd
Polmassick Vineyard Limited
Tremayne Food and Drink Ltd

**Cumbria**
Strawberry Bank Liqueurs Ltd

**Derbyshire** [6]
Amber Valley Wines Ltd
Atkinson Wines Ltd
Creative Wine Making Limited
Derbyshire Winery Limited
Rudd Farms Limited
Sloegasm Limited

**Devon** [8]
Castlewood Vineyards Ltd
Exe Valley Wines Limited
Heron Ventures Ltd
Medland Manor Vineyard Ltd.
Sharpham Partnership Limited
Sharpham Wine Limited
Silverton Wines Ltd
Torview Wines Limited

**Dorset**
Barramundi Wines Ltd
Dorchester Vineyard Limited
Furleigh Estate (Winery) Ltd
Langham Wine Limited

**Essex** [7]
Carter's Vineyards Ltd
Daavan Two Limited
Dedham Vale Vineyard Limited
Great Canney Vineyards Limited
Mersea Island Brewery & Vineyard Ltd
River Valley Vineyards Limited
Wolf Oak Limited

**Gloucestershire** [7]
Enjoy Wine Ltd
Green Ridge Wines Ltd
Kingsthorne Limited
Poulton Hill Estate Limited
Strawberry Hill Vineyard Ltd
Three Choirs Vineyards Limited
Woodchester Valley Winery Ltd

**Hampshire** [13]
Bsixtwelve Limited
Coates and Seely Limited
Danebury Vineyards Limited
Hambledon Vineyard PLC
Hambledon Wineries Limited
Hampshire Wines Limited
Hattingley Valley Wines Ltd
Itasca Wines Limited
Piersons Spirit of Wine Consulting Ltd
Rebel Pi Limited
Somborne Valley Vineyard Ltd
Vineyard Dynamics Co. Limited
Vitosha Wine Ltd

**Herefordshire**
Fair Services Limited
Global Winery Limited

**Hertfordshire** [5]
Braidclift Ltd
Globus Wines (UK) Ltd
Mosrowes Ltd
Pharos AC Ltd.
Taylor Family Wines Ltd.

**Isle of Wight**
Pure Winery Limited
Rosemary Vineyard Ltd.

**Kent** [9]
Busi-Jacobsohn Wine Estate Ltd
Chapel Down Group Ltd
Chapel Down Group PLC
English Wines PLC
Green Evolution Products Ltd
Gusbourne Estate Limited
Gusbourne PLC
Herbert Hall Wines Limited
Mereworth Wines Limited

**Lancashire** [10]
Bigmite Ltd
Chiltern Valley Liqueur Producers, Brewers & Vintners
Ben Flower Limited
Heartland Wines Europe Limited
Karmely Limited
Lakemercy Ltd
Nuclearbest Ltd
Sapphiremimic Ltd
Skinnybrands Ltd
Skyblossom Ltd

**Leicestershire**
Rothley Wine Limited
Walton Brook Vineyard Limited
Welland Valley Vineyard Ltd

**Lincolnshire**
Somerby Vineyards Limited
Stangro Limited
Witham Wines Limited

# The UK Wine Industry

**London** [56]
AB Vaults Group Limited
Able G Limited
Acloque Capital Limited
Alcohol Beverages Co Ltd
Alko Vintages UK Ltd
Arctic Wine Limited
Avanti Wines Ltd
B & F Enterprise UK Ltd
BF Wines UK Ltd
Blaxsta UK Limited
Caxdon Premier Limited
Celebrated Wines Limited
Chinese Baijiu Association Ltd
Crundale Wines Limited
Danbury Wine Estate Limited
Defined Wine Ltd
Devine Distillates Group (Manufacturing)
Digby Wine Ltd
Dropmore Vineyard Ltd
Embev Ltd
Ergene Holding (UK) Ltd.
Fiamma & Ivo Limited
Fruito Beverages (Africa) Ltd
Gavioli Ltd
General Bilimoria Wines Ltd
Green Evolution Production Ltd
K1 Beer PLC
La Remonta Limited
London Cru Ltd
Luxbev Limited
Magnus Wines Ltd
Marmoreccia Limited
Oeno Group Ltd
Pinglestone Estate Limited
Qualpro Greece Ltd.
Rockfield Wines Limited
Ross Earl Wine Co., Ltd.
San Gregorio UK Limited
Schoenlaub Limited
Silva and Cosens Limited
Simpsons Wine Estate Limited
Somm in the Must Ltd
St Emilion Holdings Limited
Sutter Home Winery Limited
Tewaina Ltd
United Manufacturing Europe Ltd
Universal Robo Innovations Ltd
Urban Initiatives Limited
Vesteraalen Vinproduksjon Ltd
Vine Revival UK Limited
Viniage Wines Limited
Weyborne Limited
Wild Life Botanicals Ltd
Wine Fusion Innovations Ltd
Winehood Ltd
World Wine Investors UK Ltd

**Merseyside**
Swift Half Collective Ltd

**Middlesex** [12]
Beringer Blass Wine Estates Ltd
Bluebell Vineyard Estates Ltd
Cellarmaster Wines Holdings (UK) Ltd
FBL Holdings Limited
James Herrick Wines Limited
New Zealand Wine Club Limited
Plummerden Estates Limited
Plummerden Lane Vineyards Ltd
Southcorp Wines Europe Limited
TWE Finance (UK) Limited
Treasury Wine Estates EMEA Ltd
Treasury Wine Estates UK Brands Ltd

**Midlothian** [6]
Direct Wine Factory Ltd
Mastropasqua & Brothers Ltd.
Our Fathers Wines Ltd
Simpsons Wine Imports Limited
Spirits Development & Management Company (SDMC)
Vergecosse Limited

**Monmouthshire**
Boutique Cellar Limited
Clandestine Distillery Limited
Lines Brew Co Ltd

**Norfolk**
Broadland Wineries Limited

**Northamptonshire**
Fleur Fields Limited
Maskstice Ltd
Nimblusher Ltd
Vinus Wine Ltd

**Northumberland**
Lindisfarne Limited

**Nottinghamshire**
Casa Vizzini Ltd

**Oxfordshire** [7]
Amwell Springs Brewery Co Ltd
Brightday Enterprises Limited
Cotswold Wine Estate Ltd
Creoda's Hill Ltd
Forgeron Dubois Limited
Santa Rita Europe Limited
Stonor Valley Winery Limited

**Powys**
Montgomery Vineyard Limited

**Shropshire**
Ghenos Vineyard Estates Ltd
Ludlow Vineyard Limited
Wroxeter Roman Vineyard Ltd

**Somerset** [6]
Bath Sparkling Wine Co Ltd
Bibelot Wine Ltd
D'Urberville Vineyard Limited
Global Wine Solutions Limited
Penselwood Partnership Ltd
Port O' Bristol Ltd

**Staffordshire**
Digby Fine English Ltd
Weinhouse Limited

**Suffolk** [7]
Casa Divertente Limited
Engstrom Group Ltd
Enlightened Entrepreneur Ltd
Flint & Vine Limited
Giffords Hall Vineyard Limited
Podere Delle Rune Ltd
Shawsgate Limited

**Surrey** [12]
Accolade Wines Limited
B & M Wines Ltd
Conradie-Penhill Wines UK Ltd.
G.I.V. UK Ltd
Greyfriars Vineyard Limited
Victor Lanson Limited
Lanson UK Limited
Leskaroon Falls Wine Estate Ltd
Little Horse Wines Limited
Realsa Wines Import & Export Ltd
South East Vineyards Association Ltd
Wines of Douro Limited

**Sussex** [34]
Albourne Winery Limited
Bach & Co Solution Limited
Beacon Down Vineyard Ltd
Black Dog Hill Estates Ltd
Bolney Vineyards Ltd
Bolney Wine Estate Ltd
Breaky Bottom Ltd
Brighton and Hove Wine Co Ltd
Carr Taylor Wines Limited
Chalk House Vineyard Limited
Court Garden Limited
Davenport Vineyards Limited
Harmony Vineyard Ltd.
Highbrook Wine Estate Limited
Kingscote Investments Limited
Kingscote Winery Ltd
Mayfield Vineyards Ltd
Nutbourne Vineyards Limited
Nyetimber (International Operations)
Nyetimber Limited
Oastbrook Estates Limited
Off The Line Limited
Ridgeview Estate Winery Ltd
Ridgeview Winery Contracts Ltd
South East Wineries Limited
Southern England Wines (UK) Ltd
Stopham Vineyard Ltd
Sugrue Pierre Limited
Sussex Vineyards Limited
Tillingham Wines Limited
Tinston Wines & Ciders Limited
UK Wine Services Limited
Upperton Vineyards Limited
Verrillo Partnership Limited

**Tyne & Wear**
Laneberg Wine Ltd
Winebar Pouch Co Ltd

**Warwickshire**
Sibling Winery Limited

**West Midlands** [5]
Amont Products Limited
Bahlina Ltd
Bathinmaestro Ltd
Gowine Limited
Selectia Wine Ltd

**Wiltshire**
A'Beckett's Vineyard Limited
Dryhill Wine Ltd
Maud Heath Wine Trading Ltd
Press Shed Wines Limited

**Worcestershire**
Aeropica Ltd

Grape Fun Limited
Sant' Elia Limited

**Yorkshire** [10]
Audiozine Ltd
Continental Wine & Food Ltd
Cool Brew Dept Ltd

De Noble Vines Limited
Eco Vino Limited
Laurel Vines, Vineyard & Winery Ltd
Noahs Estate Ltd
T & P Weinbau
Westwell Wine Estates Ltd
Yorkshire Heart Limited

# Company Profiles

**A'Beckett's Vineyard Limited**
*Incorporated:* 18 May 2000
*Net Worth:* £20,404  *Total Assets:* £87,719
*Registered Office:* A'Beckett's Farm House, High Street, Littleton Panell, Devizes, Wilts, SN10 4EN
*Major Shareholder:* Lynn Patricia Langham
*Officers:* Lynn Patricia Langham, Secretary/Legal Secretary; Lynn Patricia Langham [1962] Director/Legal Secretary; Paul Brook Langham [1964] Director/Consultant

**AB Vaults Group Limited**
*Incorporated:* 8 March 2018
*Registered Office:* 5 Academy House, 1 Thunderer Street, London, E13 9DP
*Major Shareholder:* Samuel Ndungu
*Officers:* Samuel N K Banks [1988] Director/Entrepreneur [Kenyan]

**Able G Limited**
*Incorporated:* 11 October 2018
*Registered Office:* 56 Sark Tower, Erebus Drive, London, SE28 0GG
*Officers:* Lukman Abolakale Alao [1985] Director

**Accolade Wines Limited**
*Incorporated:* 13 August 1914  *Employees:* 587
*Net Worth:* £158,856,000  *Total Assets:* £333,712,000
*Registered Office:* Thomas Hardy House, 2 Heath Road, Weybridge, Surrey, KT13 8TB
*Parent:* Accolade Brands Europe Limited
*Officers:* Anthony Graham Wood, Secretary; Adrian Francis McKeon [1963] Regional Managing Director, UKIR; Andrew Peter Smith [1974] Director/Accountant; Anthony Graham Wood [1975] Director/Financial Controller [Australian]

**Acloque Capital Limited**
*Incorporated:* 21 October 2015
*Net Worth Deficit:* £300  *Total Assets:* £100
*Registered Office:* 38 Bathurst Mews, London, W2 2SB
*Major Shareholder:* Antoine Gilles Rene Marcel Acloque
*Officers:* Antoine Acloque [1987] Director [French]; David Andrew Joynt [1977] Director/Stockbroker

**Aeropica Ltd**
*Incorporated:* 11 September 2018
*Registered Office:* Office 2, Crown House, Church Row, Pershore, Worcs, WR10 1BH
*Major Shareholder:* Andrea Marsden
*Officers:* Julius Eldrid Punzalan [1995] Director [Filipino]

**Albourne Winery Limited**
*Incorporated:* 8 July 2010  *Employees:* 1
*Net Worth:* £486,204  *Total Assets:* £660,981
*Registered Office:* Albourne Farm, Shaves Wood Lane, Albourne, Hassocks, W Sussex, BN6 9DX
*Major Shareholder:* Nicholas John Cooper
*Officers:* Dr Nicholas John Cooper [1967] Director; Alison Jane Nightingale [1966] Director

**Alcohol Beverages Company Ltd**
*Incorporated:* 15 June 2018
*Registered Office:* Pitts and Seeus, Omnibus Business Centre, 39-41 North Road, London, N7 9DP
*Major Shareholder:* James Gerald McMackin
*Officers:* James Generald McMackin [1961] Director [Irish]

**Alko Vintages UK Ltd**
*Incorporated:* 19 April 2018
*Registered Office:* 71-75 Shelton Street, Covent Garden, London, WC2H 9JQ
*Shareholders:* Archard Lwihula Kati; Elkanah Ondieki Oenga
*Officers:* Archard Lwihula Kato [1960] Director [New Zealander]; Elkanah Ondieki Oenga [1984] Director [Kenyan]

**Amber Valley Wines Ltd**
*Incorporated:* 20 April 2011
*Net Worth Deficit:* £19,655  *Total Assets:* £25,507
*Registered Office:* 2 King George Street, Wessington, Alfreton, Derbys, DE55 6DZ
*Shareholder:* Barry Lewis
*Officers:* Barry Lewis [1971] Director

**Amont Products Limited**
*Incorporated:* 5 April 2018
*Registered Office:* 36 Fentham Road, Erdington, Birmingham, B23 6AE
*Officers:* Antonio Monteiro [1959] Director/Seller [Spanish]; Elaine Moreina Valente [1967] Director/Secretary [Spanish]

**Amor Food and Beverages Holdings Limited**
*Incorporated:* 19 February 2018
*Registered Office:* 70-72 Alma Road, Windsor, Berks, SL4 3EZ
*Major Shareholder:* Craig Hodge
*Officers:* Craig Hodge [1971] Director

**Amwell Springs Brewery Company Limited**
*Incorporated:* 19 July 2017
*Net Worth Deficit:* £6,347  *Total Assets:* £33,156
*Registered Office:* Westfield Farm House, Westfield Road, Cholsey, Wallingford, Oxon, OX10 9LS
*Officers:* Andrew William Gibbons [1982] Director; David Ernest Gibbons [1951] Director; Michael David Gibbons [1979] Director; Thomas James Hammond [1982] Director; Darren Rudkin Pavitt [1967] Director

**Andreas Wine Trading Ltd**
*Incorporated:* 11 March 2015
*Net Worth:* £1,112,385  *Total Assets:* £1,158,806
*Registered Office:* 17 Lyons Fold, Sale, Cheshire, M33 6JF
*Shareholder:* David Michael Bruce Croft
*Officers:* Andrew John Bartholomew [1962] Director/Marketing Consultant; Giles Patrick Brooksbank [1957] Director of Recruitment Communications; David Michael Bruce Croft [1955] Director; David Christopher Lebond [1959] Director

**Arctic Wine Limited**
*Incorporated:* 30 August 2017
*Registered Office:* Third Floor, 207 Regent Street, London, W1B 3HH
*Parent:* Vabene Agency Limited
*Officers:* Gerhard Kolflaath [1962] Director [Norwegian]

**Atkinson Wines Ltd**
*Incorporated:* 13 March 2017  *Employees:* 2
*Net Worth:* £11,902  *Total Assets:* £41,862
*Registered Office:* 54 Windley Crescent, Darley Abbey, Derby, DE22 1BY
*Shareholders:* Kieron John Atkinson; Jane Travis
*Officers:* Kieron John Atkinson [1978] Director/Wine Maker; Jane Travis [1978] Director/Marketing

**Audiozine Ltd**
*Incorporated:* 25 June 2018
*Registered Office:* Suite 1, Fielden House, 41 Rochdale Road, Todmorden, W Yorks, OL14 6LD
*Shareholders:* Jamie Rose Feliciano; James Peace
*Officers:* Jamie Rose Feliciano [1986] Director [Filipino]

**Avanti Wines Ltd**
*Incorporated:* 11 December 2013
*Previous:* Bulles Blanc Rouge Limited
*Net Worth Deficit:* £401,871  *Total Assets:* £50,146
*Registered Office:* 3 Trebeck Street, London, W1J 7LS
*Major Shareholder:* Albert John Martin Abela
*Officers:* Albert John Martin Abela [1970] Director/Businessman

**B & F Enterprise UK Ltd**
*Incorporated:* 14 May 2018
*Registered Office:* Kemp House, 160 City Road, London, EC1V 2NX
*Officers:* Dr Olufolake Akinduro-Aje, Secretary; Benson Aje [1972] Director/Criminologist

**B & M Wines Ltd**
*Incorporated:* 7 January 2019
*Registered Office:* Ashcombe Court, Roffe Swayne, Woolsack Way, Godalming, Surrey, GU7 1LQ
*Officers:* Justin Bache [1969] Director; Kenya Matsumoto [1966] Director [Japanese]

**Bach & Co Solution Limited**
*Incorporated:* 19 December 2018
*Registered Office:* c/o Partners in Enterprise Ltd, First Floor Office, 5 Bartholomews, Brighton, BN1 1HG
*Major Shareholder:* Bachana Khachidze
*Officers:* Bachana Khachidze [1982] Director/Wine Merchant [Georgian]

**Bahlina Ltd**
*Incorporated:* 6 November 2017
*Registered Office:* 4 Equiano Place, Birmingham, B20 2FP
*Major Shareholder:* Alex Assefaw
*Officers:* Alex Assefaw [1997] Director

**Barramundi Wines Ltd**
*Incorporated:* 25 January 2017
*Registered Office:* Elmfield, Knoll Lane, Corfe Mullen, Wimborne, Dorset, BH21 3RG
*Shareholder:* John Eric Kelly
*Officers:* Christopher James Howes, Secretary; Stephen John Costley [1952] Director/Business Owner [Australian]; Dr James Lawrence Greenwood [1953] Director/Business Owner [Australian]; Gregory Iain Hutchison [1955] Director/Business Owner [Australian]; John Eric Kelly [1955] Director/Business Owner [Australian]

**Bath Sparkling Wine Company Ltd**
*Incorporated:* 16 March 2015  *Employees:* 1
*Net Worth Deficit:* £46,016  *Total Assets:* £23,735
*Registered Office:* Corston Fields Farm, Corston Fields, Corston, Bath, BA2 9EZ
*Major Shareholder:* Founder Eddie Sauvao
*Officers:* Eddie Sauvao [1975] Director/Manager; Emily Sauvao [1977] Director/Farmer

**Bathinmaestro Ltd**
*Incorporated:* 9 November 2018
*Registered Office:* Suite 16, Haldon House, Brettell Lane, Brierley Hill, W Midlands, DY5 3LQ
*Major Shareholder:* Sheridan Greenwood
*Officers:* Marlyn Del Rosario [1979] Director [Filipino]

**Beacon Down Vineyard Ltd**
*Incorporated:* 11 April 2016
*Registered Office:* 31 The Nurseries, Lewes, E Sussex, BN7 2FF
*Shareholders:* Alice Rose Pippard; Paul Sutton Pippard
*Officers:* Alice Rose Pippard [1980] Director/Local Government Officer; Paul Sutton Pippard [1977] Director/Contracting Services

**Beringer Blass Wine Estates Limited**
*Incorporated:* 7 April 1993
*Registered Office:* 9th Floor, Regal House, 70 London Road, Twickenham, Middlesex, TW1 3QS
*Parent:* Treasury Wine Estates EMEA Limited
*Officers:* Michelle Elizabeth Brampton [1972] Finance Director; Richard John Renwick [1969] Director/Chief Financial Officer Europe

**BF Wines UK Ltd**
*Incorporated:* 17 May 2018
*Registered Office:* Kemp House, 160 City Road, London, EC1V 2NX
*Officers:* Dr Olufolake Akinduro-Aje, Secretary; Benson Aje [1972] Director/Criminologist

**Bibelot Wine Ltd**
*Incorporated:* 4 December 2002
*Net Worth:* £10,263  *Total Assets:* £24,452
*Registered Office:* Higher Plot Farm, Aller Road, Langport, Somerset, TA10 0QL
*Shareholder:* Guy Christopher Smith
*Officers:* Guy Christopher Smith, Secretary; Laura Anne Evans [1962] Director; Guy Christopher Smith [1964] Director

**Bigmite Ltd**
*Incorporated:* 11 July 2018
*Registered Office:* Suite 6, First Floor, Wordsworth Mill, Wordsworth Street, Bolton, Lancs, BL1 3ND
*Major Shareholder:* Aimee Heenan
*Officers:* Anthony Pascual [1989] Director [Filipino]

**Binfield Vineyard Limited**
*Incorporated:* 24 April 2001
*Net Worth:* £1,425  *Total Assets:* £34,308
*Registered Office:* Forest Road, Wokingham, Berks, RG40 5SE
*Major Shareholder:* John Patrick Hickey
*Officers:* John Patrick Hickey [1943] Managing Director

**Black Dog Hill Estates Ltd**
*Incorporated:* 22 April 2014  *Employees:* 2
*Net Worth:* £143,200  *Total Assets:* £163,061
*Registered Office:* 30-34 North Street, Hailsham, E Sussex, BN27 1DW
*Officers:* Gunvor Birgitta Heasman [1948] Director [Swedish]; Raymond George Heasman [1945] Director; Anja Gunvor Heasman Nolan [1968] Director; James Peter Nolan [1968] Director

**Blaxsta UK Limited**
*Incorporated:* 4 January 2013
*Registered Office:* 1st Floor, 314 Regents Park Road, Finchley, London, N3 2LT
*Major Shareholder:* Goran Amnegard
*Officers:* Goran Amnegard [1958] Director [Swedish]; Lisa Alexandra Amnegard [1990] Director/Sommelier [Swedish]

### Bluebell Vineyard Estates Limited
*Incorporated:* 19 July 1982
*Net Worth Deficit:* £2,387,328  *Total Assets:* £627,579
*Registered Office:* Suite 2.8, Monument House, 215 Marsh Road, Pinner, Middlesex, HA5 5NE
*Officers:* Barry Boon Shek Tay, Secretary [Singaporean]; Andrew Hope [1956] Director/General Manager; Belinda Boon-Leen NG [1944] Director/Pharmacist [Singaporean]; Tock Sinn NG [1940] Director; Barry Boon Shek Tay [1945] Director/Biochemist; Joyce Guat Kheng Tay [1953] Director/Financial Advisor

### Boars Hill Farm Limited
*Incorporated:* 30 August 2012
*Registered Office:* 95 Hughenden Avenue, High Wycombe, Bucks, HP13 5SS
*Major Shareholder:* Vijay Singh Srao
*Officers:* Vijay Singh Srao [1965] Director

### Bolney Vineyards Ltd
*Incorporated:* 11 January 2013
*Previous:* Bolney Wine Estate Ltd
*Registered Office:* Bolney Wine Estate, Foxhole Lane, Bolney, Haywards Heath, W Sussex, RH17 5NB
*Parent:* Bolney Wine Estate Limited
*Officers:* Samantha Martha Linter [1968] Director/Wine Maker; Rodney Vince Pratt [1942] Director

### Bolney Wine Estate Ltd
*Incorporated:* 13 March 2003  *Employees:* 35
*Previous:* Bolney Wine Estate (Holdings) Ltd
*Net Worth:* £423,630  *Total Assets:* £3,276,272
*Registered Office:* Bolney Wine Estate, Foxhole Lane, Bolney, Haywards Heath, W Sussex, RH17 5NB
*Shareholders:* Greentop Investments; Samantha Martha Linter; Rodney Vince Pratt
*Officers:* Samantha Martha Linter [1968] Director/Wine Maker; Rodney Vince Pratt [1942] Director/Rubber Trader; David Derek Wood [1960] Director/Business Owner

### The Boutique Cellar Limited
*Incorporated:* 7 June 2012
*Net Worth Deficit:* £30,394  *Total Assets:* £128,656
*Registered Office:* Low Barn, Gwehelog, Usk, Monmouthshire, NP15 1HY
*Officers:* Sarah Thompson [1976] Director

### Braidclift Ltd
*Incorporated:* 18 July 2018
*Registered Office:* Ground Floor Office, 108 Fore Street, Hertford, SG14 1AB
*Major Shareholder:* Amanda Ready
*Officers:* Rosita Bagtas [1978] Director [Filipino]

### Breaky Bottom Ltd
*Incorporated:* 3 October 2013
*Net Worth Deficit:* £24
*Registered Office:* 8 High Street, Heathfield, E Sussex, TN21 8LS
*Shareholders:* Peter Anthony Inglis Hall; Christine Janet Hall
*Officers:* Christine Janet Hall [1947] Director/Wine Merchant; Peter Anthony Inglis Hall [1943] Director/Wine Merchant

### Brightday Enterprises Limited
*Incorporated:* 1 November 2002
*Net Worth:* £4  *Total Assets:* £4
*Registered Office:* Brightwell Vineyard, Rush Court, Shillingford Hill, Wallingford, Oxon, OX10 8LJ
*Shareholder:* Robert Emil Nielsen
*Officers:* Carol Nielsen, Secretary; Robert Emil Nielsen [1958] Director/Pilot

### The Brighton and Hove Wine Company Limited
*Incorporated:* 8 January 2018
*Registered Office:* 11 Colbourne Road, Hove, E Sussex, BN3 1TA
*Major Shareholder:* Brad Dyson
*Officers:* Brad Dyson [1976] Digital Director

### Broadland Wineries Limited
*Incorporated:* 15 September 1965  *Employees:* 135
*Net Worth:* £7,524,194  *Total Assets:* £24,202,070
*Registered Office:* Chapel Street, Cawston, Norwich, NR10 4BG
*Parent:* Arrhenius Holdings Ltd
*Officers:* Robert Bell [1979] Director/Chartered Accountant; Hew Richard Hamilton Dalrymple BT [1955] Director; Jonathon Mark Lansley [1962] Director/Chairman

### Bsixtwelve Limited
*Incorporated:* 7 February 2017
*Net Worth Deficit:* £20,969  *Total Assets:* £997
*Registered Office:* Lone Farm, Itchen Abbas, Winchester, Hants, SO21 1BX
*Major Shareholder:* Balbina Patricia Garcia-Benito
*Officers:* Balbina Patricia Garcia-Benito [1972] Director/Entrepreneur [Spanish]

### Busi-Jacobsohn Wine Estate Limited
*Incorporated:* 28 July 2017
*Registered Office:* Blackdon Farm, Eridge Green, Tunbridge Wells, Kent, TN3 9HX
*Shareholders:* Douglas Jacobsohn; Susanna Busi-Jacobsohn
*Officers:* Douglas Jacobsohn [1953] Director [Swedish]

### Camel Valley Limited
*Incorporated:* 13 February 2001  *Employees:* 11
*Net Worth:* £2,539,428  *Total Assets:* £2,840,769
*Registered Office:* Unit 22 Callywith Gate Industrial Estate, Launceston Road, Bodmin, Cornwall, PL31 2RQ
*Shareholders:* Anne Elizabeth Lindo; Robert Walter Lindo
*Officers:* Anne Elizabeth Lindo, Secretary; Robert Walter Lindo [1949] Director/Farmer; Samuel Robert Lindo [1976] Director/Manager

### Carr Taylor Wines Limited
*Incorporated:* 7 July 2000  *Employees:* 6
*Net Worth:* £157,916  *Total Assets:* £624,786
*Registered Office:* Carr Taylor Vineyards, Wheel Lane, Westfield, Hastings, E Sussex, TN35 4SG
*Shareholders:* David Richard Thomas Carr-Taylor; Linda Rosemary Carr-Taylor
*Officers:* David Richard Thomas Carr Taylor, Secretary; David Richard Thomas Carr Taylor [1939] Director/Wine Grower; Linda Rosemary Carr Taylor [1945] Director/Wine Grower

### Carter's Vineyards Ltd
*Incorporated:* 5 April 2012  *Employees:* 5
*Net Worth Deficit:* £144,921  *Total Assets:* £106,499
*Registered Office:* Carter's Vineyards Ltd, Green Lane, Boxted, Colchester, Essex, CO4 5TS
*Major Shareholder:* Thomas William Bunting
*Officers:* Thomas William Bunting [1977] Director/Vineyard Management

### Casa Divertente Limited
*Incorporated:* 23 January 2017
*Net Worth:* £1,921  *Total Assets:* £48,737
*Registered Office:* Flint Cottage, 25 High Rougham, Bury St Edmunds, Suffolk, IP30 9LN
*Shareholders:* Janette Anne Steel; James Ian Steel
*Officers:* James Ian Steel, Secretary; James Ian Steel [1944] Director/Retired; Janette Anne Steel [1949] Director/Retired

**Casa Vizzini Ltd**
*Incorporated:* 1 April 2016
*Net Worth Deficit:* £706  *Total Assets:* £330,300
*Registered Office:* Mercury House, Shipstones Business Center, North Gate, Nottingham, NG7 7FN
*Officers:* Peter Robson, Secretary; Peter Robson [1959] Director

**Castlewood Vineyards Ltd**
*Incorporated:* 5 February 2016  *Employees:* 1
*Net Worth:* £1,218  *Total Assets:* £49,893
*Registered Office:* Castlewood Farm, Musbury, Axminster, Devon, EX13 8SS
*Major Shareholder:* Robert Henry Corbett
*Officers:* Robert Henry Corbett [1983] Director

**Caxdon Premier Limited**
*Incorporated:* 21 July 2017
*Registered Office:* 14-16 Powis Street, London, SE18 6LF
*Major Shareholder:* Donald Toseafa
*Officers:* Caroline Toseafa [1969] Director/Healthcare Practitioner; Donald Toseafa [1962] Director/Psychiatric Practitioner

**Celebrated Wines Limited**
*Incorporated:* 1 September 2016
*Net Worth:* £1  *Total Assets:* £1
*Registered Office:* Newcombe House, 43-45 Notting Hill Gate, London, W11 3LQ
*Major Shareholder:* Mark Morris
*Officers:* Mark Morris [1988] Director

**Cellarmaster Wines Holdings (UK) Limited**
*Incorporated:* 29 January 1968
*Net Worth:* £29,715,000  *Total Assets:* £29,715,000
*Registered Office:* 9th Floor, Regal House, 70 London Road, Twickenham, Middlesex, TW1 3QS
*Officers:* Michelle Elizabeth Brampton [1972] Finance Director; Richard John Renwick [1969] Director/Chief Financial Officer Europe

**Chalk House Vineyard Limited**
*Incorporated:* 12 October 2012  *Employees:* 1
*Previous:* Flints Vineyard Limited
*Net Worth Deficit:* £39,984  *Total Assets:* £1,493,054
*Registered Office:* 30-34 North Street, Hailsham, E Sussex, BN27 1DW
*Shareholders:* Ben Ellis; Samantha Ellis
*Officers:* Benjamin Paul Ellis [1972] Director/Town Planner; Samantha Ellis [1973] Director

**Chapel Down Group Ltd**
*Incorporated:* 26 May 2011
*Registered Office:* Chapel Down Winery, Small Hythe Road, Tenterden, Kent, TN30 7NG
*Parent:* Chapel Down Group PLC
*Officers:* Richard Alexander Bruce Woodhouse [1973] Director/Chartered Accountant

**Chapel Down Group PLC**
*Incorporated:* 28 January 2002  *Employees:* 60
*Net Worth:* £33,914,892  *Total Assets:* £39,469,820
*Registered Office:* Chapel Down Winery, Smallhythe Road, Tenterden, Kent, TN30 7NG
*Shareholder:* IPGL Limited
*Officers:* Richard Alexander Bruce Woodhouse, Secretary/Chartered Accountant; Gareth Bath [1978] Managing Director; James Dominic Brooke [1971] Director/Investment Manager; John Michael Dunsmore [1959] Director; Selina Holliday Emeny [1968] Director/Lawyer; Mark Simon Harvey [1976] Director; Frazer Douglas Thompson [1959] Managing Director; Richard Alexander Bruce Woodhouse [1973] Director/Chartered Accountant; Nigel William Wray [1948] Director

**Chiltern Valley Liqueur Producers, Brewers & Vintners Ltd.**
*Incorporated:* 23 December 2014
*Net Worth:* £1,627  *Total Assets:* £185,379
*Registered Office:* Suite 307, 76 King Street, Manchester, M2 4NH
*Shareholders:* David Ealand; Donald Arthur Ealand; Duncan Fortune Ealand; Olivia Clare Ealand
*Officers:* Donald Arthur Ealand [1984] Director; Duncan Fortune Ealand [1982] Director; Olivia Clare Ealand [1980] Director

**Chinese Baijiu Association Ltd**
*Incorporated:* 22 January 2018
*Registered Office:* 38 Portland Road, London, SE25 4PF
*Officers:* Tong Zhu [1980] Director/Property Developer [Chinese]

**The Clandestine Distillery Limited**
*Incorporated:* 21 December 2018
*Registered Office:* Low Barn, Llancayo Business Park, Usk, Monmouthshire, NP15 1HY
*Shareholders:* Nathan Edward Thompson; Sarah Thompson
*Officers:* Nathan Edward Thompson [1978] Director

**Coates and Seely Limited**
*Incorporated:* 19 August 2008  *Employees:* 3
*Net Worth Deficit:* £435,826  *Total Assets:* £1,891,802
*Registered Office:* Wooldings Vineyard, Harroway, Whitchurch, Hants, RG28 7QT
*Shareholders:* Christian James Russell Seely; Northington Advisors Limited
*Officers:* Nicholas Bloy [1962] Director/Investment Management; Nicholas John Coates [1959] Director; Michael Potter Saunders [1963] Director/CEO - Bibendum PLB; Christian James Russell Seely [1960] Director

**Conradie-Penhill Wines UK Ltd.**
*Incorporated:* 17 March 2015
*Net Worth Deficit:* £67,106  *Total Assets:* £4,911
*Registered Office:* 1 Tudors Business Centre, Station Yard, Waterhouse Lane, Kingswood, Tadworth, Surrey, KT20 6EN
*Officers:* Kate Huntsman Penny [1967] Director

**Continental Wine & Food Limited**
*Incorporated:* 28 December 1960  *Employees:* 214
*Net Worth:* £26,940,560  *Total Assets:* £37,602,080
*Registered Office:* Trafalgar Mills, Leeds Road, Huddersfield, W Yorks, HD2 1YY
*Shareholder:* Alessandro Bevilacqua
*Officers:* Peter John Taylor, Secretary/Accountant; Alessandro Bevilacqua [1955] Director [Italian]; John David Shinwell [1964] Development Director; Peter John Taylor [1957] Financial Director

**Cool Brew Dept Ltd**
*Incorporated:* 26 June 2018
*Registered Office:* Flat 2, 134 Valley Drive, Harrogate, N Yorks, HG2 0JS
*Major Shareholder:* Matthew Leonard Edgar
*Officers:* Matthew Leonard Edgar [1984] Director

**Cotswold Wine Estate Ltd**
*Incorporated:* 15 November 2018
*Registered Office:* 2 Stopford Place, Chipping Norton, Oxon, OX7 5SL
*Shareholders:* Jasper Orlando Pye; George William Clarke
*Officers:* George William Clarke [1997] Director/Brewer; Patrick Charles Stewart Marriot [1997] Director/Wine Retail; Jasper Orlando Pye [1997] Director/Artist

**Court Garden Limited**
*Incorporated:* 4 February 1977
*Net Worth:* £115,791  *Total Assets:* £576,503
*Registered Office:* 1 West Street, Lewes, E Sussex, BN7 2NZ
*Shareholders:* William Howard Corney; Jennifer Lynn Corney; Hugo Corney
*Officers:* Jennifer Lynn Corney, Secretary; Hugo Corney [1975] Director; Jennifer Lynn Corney [1949] Director; William Howard Corney [1949] Director


**Michel Couvreur (Scotch Whiskies) Limited**
*Incorporated:* 22 April 1988  *Employees:* 6
*Net Worth:* £1,514,178  *Total Assets:* £2,077,092
*Registered Office:* Meldrum House, Old Meldrum, Aberdeenshire, AB5 0AE
*Parent:* Al Spirit
*Officers:* Marthe Georgette Andree Couvreur [1932] Director [French]; Alexandra Marie Elisabeth Deschamps [1972] Director/Housewife [French]; Cyril Deschamps [1973] Director [French]; Jean Arnaud Frantzen [1973] Director [French]


**Creative Wine Making Limited**
*Incorporated:* 19 February 2014  *Employees:* 3
*Net Worth:* £85,366  *Total Assets:* £189,619
*Registered Office:* Unit 1 Plot 14, Eagle Road, Ilkeston, Derbys, DE7 4RB
*Major Shareholder:* Samuel David Robinson
*Officers:* Pamela Joy Robinson [1957] Director; Peter William Robinson [1952] Director; Samuel David Robinson [1985] Director


**Creoda's Hill Ltd**
*Incorporated:* 9 February 2016  *Employees:* 1
*Net Worth Deficit:* £2,447  *Total Assets:* £5,509
*Registered Office:* Horse Shoe House, Horse Shoe Lane, Wootton, Woodstock, Oxon, OX20 1DR
*Major Shareholder:* Matthew Bennett Rippon
*Officers:* Matthew Bennett Rippon [1968] Director


**Crundale Wines Limited**
*Incorporated:* 10 July 2017
*Net Worth:* £100  *Total Assets:* £100
*Registered Office:* 8 Godwin Road, London, E7 0LE
*Major Shareholder:* Thomas David Hewson
*Officers:* Thomas David Hewson, Secretary; Thomas David Hewson [1985] Director/Musician


**D'Urberville Vineyard Limited**
*Incorporated:* 23 November 2016  *Employees:* 1
*Net Worth:* £1  *Total Assets:* £42,492
*Registered Office:* Mary Street House, Mary Street, Taunton, Somerset, TA1 3NW
*Major Shareholder:* Colin Charles Hawkins
*Officers:* Colin Charles Hawkins [1950] Director/Agriculture


**Daavan Two Limited**
*Incorporated:* 7 January 2019
*Registered Office:* 39 Hildaville Drive, Westcliff on Sea, Essex, SS0 9RU
*Major Shareholder:* Weiqing Hu
*Officers:* Weiqing Hu [1991] Director/Doorman [Chinese]


**Danbury Wine Estate Limited**
*Incorporated:* 12 November 2012
*Previous:* Bunkers Vineyards Limited
*Net Worth Deficit:* £299,954  *Total Assets:* £1,584,899
*Registered Office:* Lower Ground Floor, 14 Devonshire Square, London, EC2M 4YT
*Shareholders:* Michael Stewart Bunker; Heather Ellen Bunker; Sophie Louise Bunker; Janine Heather Hurley
*Officers:* Heather Ellen Bunker, Secretary; Heather Bunker [1953] Director; Michael Stewart Bunker [1950] Director


**Danebury Vineyards Limited**
*Incorporated:* 11 June 1993  *Employees:* 4
*Net Worth Deficit:* £1,848,697  *Total Assets:* £205,385
*Registered Office:* c/o Messrs Martin & Company, 25 St Thomas Street, Winchester, Hants, SO23 9DD
*Shareholders:* Sebastian Piech; Florian Piech; Charlotte Wanivenhaus
*Officers:* Patrick Jonathan Ralph Westropp, Secretary; Florian Piech [1962] Director/Venture Capital Manager [Austrian]; Charlotte Wainvenhaus [1960] Director [Austrian]


**Davenport Vineyards Limited**
*Incorporated:* 27 June 2017
*Registered Office:* Limney Farm, Castle Hill, Rotherfield, E Sussex, TN6 3RR
*Shareholders:* Louisa Kate Arabella Belli; William Talbot John Davenport
*Officers:* Louisa Kate Arabella Belli [1969] Sales Director; William Talbot John Davenport [1964] Director/Winemaker; Philip Lewis Harris [1982] Director/Vineyard Manager


**De Noble Vines Limited**
*Incorporated:* 4 July 2007
*Net Worth Deficit:* £6,734  *Total Assets:* £1,350
*Registered Office:* Heritage Exchange, South Lane, Elland, W Yorks, HX5 0HG
*Major Shareholder:* Laurence David Noble
*Officers:* Laurence David Noble, Secretary; Laurence David Noble [1957] Director/IT Manager


**Dedham Vale Vineyard Limited**
*Incorporated:* 20 November 2012
*Net Worth Deficit:* £97,001  *Total Assets:* £302,745
*Registered Office:* The Vineyard, Green Lane, Boxted, Colchester, Essex, CO4 5TS
*Shareholders:* Janice Wilson; Michael William Roberts
*Officers:* Michael William Roberts [1948] Director; Janice Wilson [1953] Director/Interior Designer [Australian]


**Defined Wine Ltd**
*Incorporated:* 26 November 2018
*Registered Office:* Lower Ground Floor, 4-5 Gough Square, London, EC4A 3DE
*Officers:* Henry Sugden, Secretary; Henry Francis Austin Sugden [1966] Director


**The Derbyshire Winery Limited**
*Incorporated:* 21 October 2010
*Net Worth:* £4,120  *Total Assets:* £20,023
*Registered Office:* Unit 13a Riverside Business Park, Buxton Road, Bakewell, Derbys, DE45 1GS
*Major Shareholder:* Keith Hugh Daily
*Officers:* Keith Hugh Daily [1960] Director

**Devine Distillates Group (Manufacturing) Ltd**
*Incorporated:* 14 September 2018
*Registered Office:* 71-75 Shelton Street, Covent Garden, London, WC2H 9JQ
*Shareholders:* Peter Joseph Robson; Loch Shiel Whisky Ltd
*Officers:* Peter Joseph Robson, Secretary; Peter Joseph Robson [1959] Director


**Deviock Wine Company Limited**
*Incorporated:* 3 May 2007
*Net Worth Deficit:* £841,560  *Total Assets:* £676,696
*Registered Office:* Knightor Manor, Trethurgy, St Austell, Cornwall, PL26 8YQ
*Officers:* Annya Christine Derx, Secretary; Adrian William Derx [1960] Director


**Digby Fine English Ltd**
*Incorporated:* 5 April 2012
*Net Worth:* £1,218,131  *Total Assets:* £1,218,131
*Registered Office:* c/o DPC, Vernon Road, Stoke on Trent, Staffs, ST4 2QY
*Shareholders:* Trevor Todd Clough; Jason John Humphries
*Officers:* Ewen Irving Cameron [1956] Director; Trevor Todd Clough [1975] Director; Dr Jason John Humphries [1971] Director; Weicheng Zhang [1989] Director [Chinese]


**Digby Wine Ltd**
*Incorporated:* 5 April 2012  *Employees:* 4
*Net Worth Deficit:* £431,322  *Total Assets:* £1,219,494
*Registered Office:* 1 Berkeley Street, Mayfair, London, W1J 8DJ
*Parent:* Digby Fine English Ltd
*Officers:* Ewen Irving Cameron [1956] Director; Trevor Todd Clough [1975] Director; Dr Jason John Humphries [1971] Director; Weicheng Zhang [1989] Director [Chinese]


**Dinton Wines Limited**
*Incorporated:* 23 July 2013
*Net Worth Deficit:* £25,745  *Total Assets:* £44,854
*Registered Office:* Willow End, Upton Road, Upton, Aylesbury, Bucks, HP17 8UF
*Major Shareholder:* Lawrence George Kimber
*Officers:* Lawrence George Kimber [1934] Director/Retired


**Direct Wine Factory Ltd**
*Incorporated:* 12 June 2013
*Previous:* Wine Factory Direct Ltd
*Net Worth:* £2,174,676  *Total Assets:* £2,174,676
*Registered Office:* Mitchell House, Mitchell Street, Edinburgh, EH6 7BD


**Dorchester Vineyard Limited**
*Incorporated:* 14 December 2012
*Net Worth:* £100  *Total Assets:* £100
*Registered Office:* 14a Albany Road, Weymouth, Dorset, DT4 9TH
*Major Shareholder:* Nichola Clare Prowse
*Officers:* Nichola Clare Prowse [1964] Director; Nicholas Prowse [1969] Director


**Drinktonics Limited**
*Incorporated:* 18 December 2018
*Registered Office:* Trevella Manor, Trispen, Truro, Cornwall, TR4 9BD
*Major Shareholder:* Anne-Marie Hurst
*Officers:* Anne-Marie Hurst [1965] Director


**Dropmore Vineyard Ltd**
*Incorporated:* 20 November 2018
*Registered Office:* 1 Kings Avenue, London, N21 3NA
*Major Shareholder:* Feona Mary McEwan
*Officers:* Feona Mary McEwan [1950] Director


**Dryhill Wine Ltd**
*Incorporated:* 21 April 2016
*Net Worth Deficit:* £34,805  *Total Assets:* £5,521
*Registered Office:* 38-42 Newport Street, Swindon, Wilts, SN1 3DR
*Shareholders:* Lesley Anne Rowley; Nigel Graham Rowley
*Officers:* Lesley Anne Rowley [1957] Director; Nigel Graham Rowley [1958] Director


**Duncairn Wines Limited**
*Incorporated:* 6 April 1965  *Employees:* 16
*Net Worth:* £441,437  *Total Assets:* £1,188,302
*Registered Office:* 5-7 Corporation Square, Belfast, BT1 3AJ
*Shareholders:* Peter McAlindon; Neal Edward McAlindon
*Officers:* Maureen Sarah McAlindon, Secretary; Kevin Peter McAlindon [1965] Director/Wine Merchant; Neal Edward McAlindon [1969] Director/Wine Buyer


**Eco Vino Limited**
*Incorporated:* 2 April 2013
*Registered Office:* Belfast House, 6a Bingley Road, Saltaire, Bradford, W Yorks, BD18 4RJ
*Officers:* Joanne Elizabeth Lee [1977] Director


**Embev Ltd**
*Incorporated:* 16 May 2018
*Registered Office:* Flat 3, 162 Cambridge Street, London, SW1V 4QE
*Major Shareholder:* Matthew Nicolas Clark
*Officers:* Matthew Nicolas Clark [1990] Director/Entrepreneur


**Enborne Vineyards Limited**
*Incorporated:* 22 November 2011
*Net Worth Deficit:* £74,667  *Total Assets:* £338,224
*Registered Office:* Church Farm, Enborne, Berks, RG20 0HD
*Major Shareholder:* Mark Leonard Darley
*Officers:* Mark Leonard Darley [1961] Director/Solicitor


**English Wines PLC**
*Incorporated:* 25 April 2000  *Employees:* 60
*Net Worth:* £1,510,986  *Total Assets:* £9,769,827
*Registered Office:* Chapel Down Winery, Smallhythe Road, Tenterden, Kent, TN30 7NG
*Parent:* Chapel Down Group PLC
*Officers:* Richard Alexander Bruce Woodhouse, Secretary/Chartered Accountant; Frazer Douglas Thompson [1959] Managing Director; Richard Alexander Bruce Woodhouse [1973] Director/Chartered Accountant


**Engstrom Group Ltd**
*Incorporated:* 16 May 2018
*Registered Office:* First Floor Suite, 2 Hillside Business Park, Bury St Edmunds, Suffolk, IP32 7EA
*Major Shareholder:* Hans Ivan Engstrom
*Officers:* Hans Ivan Engstrom [1959] Director [Swedish]


**Enjoy Wine Ltd**
*Incorporated:* 8 August 2009
*Registered Office:* Walton Cardiff Manor, Walton Cardiff, Tewkesbury, Glos, GL20 7BL
*Officers:* Henry Alistair Samuel Sandbach, Secretary; Henry Alistair Samuel Sandbach [1944] Director/Wine Merchant

**Enlightened Entrepreneur Ltd**
*Incorporated:* 24 April 2017
*Registered Office:* 49 Stoney Road, Grundisburgh, Woodbridge, Suffolk, IP13 6RQ
*Shareholders:* Thomas Huw Hepworth-Bond; James Thomson Farquhar
*Officers:* James Thomson Farquhar [1989] Director; Thomas Huw Hepworth-Bond [1988] Director

**Ergene Holding (UK) Ltd.**
*Incorporated:* 19 January 2009
*Registered Office:* 18c The Broadway, West Ealing, London, W13 0SR
*Officers:* Ergenekon Mustafa Avci, Secretary; Ergenekon Mustafa Avci [1973] Director/Company Owner

**Evremond Estate Limited**
*Incorporated:* 27 April 2015
*Net Worth:* £4,079,277  *Total Assets:* £4,366,007
*Registered Office:* New Bank House, 1 Brockenhurst Road, Ascot, Berks, SL5 9DJ
*Parent:* Taittinger C.C.V.C
*Officers:* Paul Andrew Hughes-D'aeth, Secretary; The Honourable James Henry Morys Bruce [1948] Director; Lord Charles Generald John Cadogan [1937] Director; Damien Bruno Paul Marie Le Sueur [1975] Director [French]; Patrick William McGrath [1960] Director/Wine Merchant; Clovis Taittinger [1978] Director [French]; Pierre-Emmanuel Taittinger [1953] Director [French]

**Evremond Vineyards Limited**
*Incorporated:* 13 February 2018
*Registered Office:* New Bank House, Brockenhurst Road, Ascot, Berks, SL5 9DJ
*Major Shareholder:* Patrick William McGrath
*Officers:* Paul Andrew Hughes D'Aeth [1962] Director

**Exe Valley Wines Limited**
*Incorporated:* 18 June 2002
*Net Worth:* £1,740  *Total Assets:* £12,691
*Registered Office:* Yearlstone Vineyard, Bickleigh, Tiverton, Devon, EX16 8RL
*Shareholder:* Juliet Anne White
*Officers:* Roger Julian White, Secretary; Juliet Anne White [1962] Director/Winemaker

**Fair Services Limited**
*Incorporated:* 9 September 1998
*Net Worth:* £57,451  *Total Assets:* £96,575
*Registered Office:* The Vineyard Cottage, Symonds Yat, Ross on Wye, Herefords, HR9 6BW
*Officers:* Glynis Eileen Cozens, Secretary; Glynis Eileen Cozens [1945] Director/Secretary

**FBL Holdings Limited**
*Incorporated:* 20 June 2008
*Net Worth Deficit:* £30,647,000  *Total Assets:* £75,101,000
*Registered Office:* 9th Floor, Regal House, 70 London Road, Twickenham, Middlesex, TW1 3QS
*Parent:* Treasury Wine Estates EMEA Limited
*Officers:* Michelle Elizabeth Brampton [1972] Finance Director; Richard John Renwick [1969] Director/Chief Financial Officer Europe

**Fiamma & Ivo Limited**
*Incorporated:* 10 May 2013
*Net Worth Deficit:* £7,533  *Total Assets:* £61,430
*Registered Office:* 34-35 Eastcastle Street, London, W1W 8DW
*Shareholders:* Ivailo Varbanov; Fiammetta Tarli
*Officers:* Fiammetta Tarli [1970] Director/Music & Wine

**Fleur Fields Limited**
*Incorporated:* 27 August 2002
*Net Worth:* £62,569  *Total Assets:* £99,858
*Registered Office:* Hill Farm House, Northampton Road, Brixworth, Northants, NN6 9DQ
*Shareholders:* William Allen Hulme; Flora Elsie Hulme
*Officers:* William Allen Hulme, Secretary; Flora Elsie Hulme [1946] Director/Wine Grower; William Allen Hulme [1942] Director/Accountant

**Flint & Vine Limited**
*Incorporated:* 19 June 2015
*Net Worth Deficit:* £22,558  *Total Assets:* £193,259
*Registered Office:* Camp Hill Farm, Middle Road, Earsham, Bungay, Suffolk, NR35 2AH
*Shareholders:* Benjamin James Witchell; Hannah Mary Witchell; Adrian Paul Hipwell
*Officers:* Adrian Paul Hipwell [1958] Director/Farmer; Benjamin James Witchell [1975] Director/Wine Maker; Hannah Mary Witchell [1980] Director

**Ben Flower Limited**
*Incorporated:* 12 April 2018
*Registered Office:* 12 Northland Road, Manchester, M9 7AG
*Officers:* Ben Thackeray [1982] Director/Retail

**The Flower Miners Limited**
*Incorporated:* 8 January 2019
*Registered Office:* Trevella, Trispen, Truro, Cornwall, TR4 9BD
*Major Shareholder:* Anne-Marie Hurst
*Officers:* Anne-Marie Hurst [1965] Director

**Forgeron Dubois Limited**
*Incorporated:* 14 June 2016
*Registered Office:* Rose Cottage, Church Hanborough, Witney, Oxon, OX29 8AA
*Officers:* James Fleetwood [1965] Director/Wine Importer; Timothy James Smith [1964] Managing Director

**Fruito Beverages (Africa) Limited**
*Incorporated:* 23 July 2018
*Registered Office:* 65 Samuel Street, London, SE18 5LF
*Parent:* Fruito (UK) Limited
*Officers:* Adekunle Akanji Ademola [1955] Director/Consultant

**Furleigh Estate (Winery) Ltd**
*Incorporated:* 29 March 2011
*Net Worth:* £66,153  *Total Assets:* £71,784
*Registered Office:* Furleigh Farm, Salwayash, Bridport, Dorset, DT6 5JF
*Shareholders:* Ian Edwards; Rebecca Ruth Hansford
*Officers:* Ian Edwards [1955] Director/Vineyard Owner; Rebecca Ruth Hansford [1963] Director/Vineyard Owner

**G.I.V. UK Ltd**
*Incorporated:* 28 July 1997  *Employees:* 3
*Net Worth:* £122,828  *Total Assets:* £281,217
*Registered Office:* Gladstone House, 77-79 High Street, Egham, Surrey, TW20 9HY
*Officers:* Roberta Corra [1972] Managing Director [Italian]; Maria Elena Fossati [1967] Director [Italian]; Marco Gobbi [1959] Director [Italian]

**Gavioli Ltd**
*Incorporated:* 9 January 2019
*Registered Office:* 20 Hornton Street, Kensington, London, W8 4NR
*Shareholders:* Grahame McGirr; Giuseppe Martorana
*Officers:* Giuseppe Martorana [1953] Director [Italian]; Grahame McGirr [1977] Director

**General Bilimoria Wines Limited**
*Incorporated:* 28 January 2009
*Net Worth:* £5,295  *Total Assets:* £152,257
*Registered Office:* 1 Doughty Street, London, WC1N 2PH
*Shareholders:* Karan Faridoon Bilimoria; Lady Lynne Heather Bilimoria
*Officers:* Lord Karan Faridoon Bilimoria [1961] Director

**Ghenos Vineyard Estates Ltd**
*Incorporated:* 20 October 2017
*Registered Office:* 6 Claremont Buildings, Claremont Bank, Shrewsbury, Salop, SY1 1RJ
*Shareholders:* Andrew Charles Stevens; Dora Stevens
*Officers:* Andrew Charles Stevens [1959] Director; Dora Stevens [1958] Director [Malaysian]

**Giffords Hall Vineyard Limited**
*Incorporated:* 30 March 2012  *Employees:* 4
*Net Worth:* £533,339  *Total Assets:* £646,085
*Registered Office:* Giffords Hall, Shimpling, Bury St Edmunds, Suffolk, IP29 4EX
*Shareholders:* Guy Halsall Howard; Catherine Linda Howard
*Officers:* Catherine Linda Howard [1963] Director; Guy Halsall Howard [1957] Director

**Global Wine Solutions Limited**
*Incorporated:* 20 October 2016
*Net Worth:* £34,667  *Total Assets:* £120,305
*Registered Office:* Park House, 10 Park Street, Bristol, BS1 5HX
*Major Shareholder:* Liam Liam Steevenson
*Officers:* Liam James Steevenson [1975] Director/Wine Merchant

**The Global Winery Limited**
*Incorporated:* 9 May 2002  *Employees:* 6
*Net Worth Deficit:* £307,374  *Total Assets:* £1,034,675
*Registered Office:* The Bounds, Much Marcle, Ledbury, Herefords, HR8 2NQ
*Parent:* H Weston & Sons Ltd
*Officers:* Patrick Matthew Smith, Secretary; Martin Hoult Fowke [1962] Director; David Griffiths [1963] Director; Patrick Matthew Smith [1966] Director; Helen Maureen Thomas [1953] Company Director

**Globus Wines (UK) Ltd**
*Incorporated:* 7 August 2009
*Net Worth:* £36,697  *Total Assets:* £191,132
*Registered Office:* 9 Parkfield, Chorleywood, Rickmansworth, Herts, WD3 5AY
*Major Shareholder:* Aashima Hariyani
*Officers:* Aashima Hariyani [1978] Director

**Gowine Limited**
*Incorporated:* 11 February 1997  *Employees:* 12
*Net Worth:* £508,816  *Total Assets:* £878,195
*Registered Office:* The Vineyards, Tom Lane, Bobbington, Stourbridge, W Midlands, DY7 5EP
*Shareholders:* Clive Martin Charles Vickers; Martin Charles Vickers
*Officers:* Lisa Christine Vickers, Secretary; Clive Martin Charles Vickers [1967] Director/Viticulturist

**Grape Fun Limited**
*Incorporated:* 3 January 2018
*Registered Office:* Shoulton House Farm, Shoulton, Hallow, Worcs, WR2 6PX
*Shareholders:* James Deakin; Jonathon David Charles Tainton
*Officers:* James Deakin [1975] Director; Jonathon David Charles Tainton [1964] Director

**Great Canney Vineyards Limited**
*Incorporated:* 7 December 2016
*Net Worth Deficit:* £10,951  *Total Assets:* £17,967
*Registered Office:* Unit L, Radford Business Centre, Radford Way, Billericay, Essex, CM12 0BZ
*Shareholders:* Daniel Stephen; Tom Stephen
*Officers:* Daniel Stephen [1982] Director; Tom Stephen [1985] Director

**Green Evolution Production Ltd**
*Incorporated:* 21 January 2019
*Registered Office:* 71-75 Shelton Street, London, WC2H 9JQ
*Major Shareholder:* Stephanie French
*Officers:* Stephanie French, Secretary; Stephanie French [1988] Director

**Green Evolution Products Ltd**
*Incorporated:* 5 October 2018
*Registered Office:* Provident House, Burrell Row, Beckenham, Kent, BR3 1AT
*Major Shareholder:* Antony Granger
*Officers:* John Badham [1980] Director; Antony Granger [1981] Director

**Green Ridge Wines Ltd**
*Incorporated:* 19 September 2014
*Net Worth:* £62,060  *Total Assets:* £332,452
*Registered Office:* Goodridge Court, Goodridge Avenue, Gloucester, GL2 5EN
*Shareholders:* Martin Hoult Fowke; Elaine Frances Fowke
*Officers:* Elaine Frances Fowke [1964] Director

**Greyfriars Vineyard Limited**
*Incorporated:* 5 October 2010  *Employees:* 11
*Net Worth Deficit:* £976,749  *Total Assets:* £4,632,057
*Registered Office:* The Hogs Back, Puttenham, Guildford, Surrey, GU3 1AG
*Shareholders:* Hilary Mary Wagstaff; Michael John Wagstaff
*Officers:* Hilary Mary Wagstaff [1962] Director; Michael John Wagstaff [1961] Director

**Guinexport Trade and Services Limited**
*Incorporated:* 3 November 2014
*Net Worth Deficit:* £13,789  *Total Assets:* £1,872
*Registered Office:* 7 Venus Way, Peterborough, Cambs, PE2 8GF
*Major Shareholder:* Dionisio Bisan-Etame Mayer
*Officers:* Dionisio Bisan-Etame Mayer [1969] Director/Trader [Spanish]

**Gusbourne Estate Limited**
*Incorporated:* 10 June 2011  *Employees:* 21
*Net Worth Deficit:* £3,718,589  *Total Assets:* £16,207,621
*Registered Office:* Gusbourne Estate, Kenardington Road, Appledore, Kent, TN26 2BE
*Parent:* Gusbourne PLC
*Officers:* Ian George Robinson [1947] Director; Andrew Carl Vincent Weeber [1946] Director [South African]

**Gusbourne PLC**
*Incorporated:* 24 September 2012  *Employees:* 25
*Net Worth:* £12,330,000  *Total Assets:* £17,466,000
*Registered Office:* Gusbourne, Kenardington Road, Appledore, Ashford, Kent, TN26 2BE
*Major Shareholder:* Michael Ashcroft
*Officers:* Ian George Robinson, Secretary; Baron James Norwich Arbuthnot [1952] Director/Consultant; Paul Generald Bentham [1960] Director; Matthew David Clapp [1979] Director/Consultant; Charles Edward Holland [1977] Director; Michael Anthony Keyes Paul [1948] Director; Jonathan David Pollard [1976] Director; Ian George Robinson [1947] Director; Andrew Carl Vincent Weeber [1946] Director [South African]


**Gwinllan Conwy Ltd**
*Incorporated:* 15 March 2016
*Net Worth:* £11,443  *Total Assets:* £38,436
*Registered Office:* Y Gwinwydd, Llangwstenin, Llandudno Junction, Conwy, LL31 9JF
*Officers:* Charlotte Louise Bennett [1978] Managing Director; Colin Stephen Bennett [1959] Director


**Herbert Hall Wines Limited**
*Incorporated:* 12 September 2007
*Net Worth Deficit:* £22,616  *Total Assets:* £221,504
*Registered Office:* 74 College Road, Maidstone, Kent, ME15 6SL
*Major Shareholder:* Nicholas Morton Hall
*Officers:* Catherine Miranda Hall, Secretary; Nicholas Morton Hall [1959] Director


**Hambledon Vineyard PLC**
*Incorporated:* 24 November 2010  *Employees:* 19
*Net Worth:* £760,222  *Total Assets:* £5,263,902
*Registered Office:* The Vineyard, East Street, Hambledon, Waterlooville, Hants, PO7 4RY
*Major Shareholder:* Ian James Kellett
*Officers:* Graham Alan Jeffs, Secretary; Steven Andrew Blakey [1959] Director; Andrew William Michael Christie-Miller [1950] Director/Farmer; Ian James Kellett [1965] Director; William Martin Robinson [1958] Director


**Hambledon Wineries Limited**
*Incorporated:* 16 October 2009  *Employees:* 19
*Net Worth Deficit:* £2,040,846  *Total Assets:* £5,236,812
*Registered Office:* The Vineyard, East Street, Hambledon, Waterlooville, Hants, PO7 4RY
*Major Shareholder:* Ian James Kellett
*Officers:* Graham Alan Jeffs, Secretary; Steven Andrew Blakey [1959] Director; Andrew William Michael Christie-Miller [1950] Director/Farmer; Ian James Kellett [1965] Director/Wine Grower; William Martin Robinson [1958] Director/Chartered Accountant


**Hampshire Wines Limited**
*Incorporated:* 13 June 2011
*Registered Office:* 3 Payne's Place, Hedge End, Southampton, SO30 2LS
*Shareholders:* Sunil Arora; Dennis Balcombe
*Officers:* Sunil Arora [1965] Director/Investment Banker; Dennis Balcombe [1959] Project Manager (Director)


**Harmony Vineyard Ltd.**
*Incorporated:* 28 July 2016
*Registered Office:* 5 Kings Court, Beach Green, Shoreham-by-Sea, W Sussex, BN43 5YD
*Shareholder:* Bernard John West
*Officers:* Dr Bernard John West [1947] Director/Viticulturist; Fiona West [1958] Director/Viticulturist


**Harrow & Hope Limited**
*Incorporated:* 1 April 2003  *Employees:* 2
*Previous:* H. J. H Barrel Wines Limited
*Net Worth Deficit:* £308,681  *Total Assets:* £1,254,141
*Registered Office:* Marlow Winery, Pump Lane North, Marlow, Bucks, SL7 3RD
*Major Shareholder:* Henry John Hugh Laithwaite
*Officers:* Kaye Louise Laithwaite, Secretary; Henry John Hugh Laithwaite [1980] Director/Wine Merchant; Kaye Louise Laithwaite [1980] Director/General Manager


**Hattingley Valley Wines Limited**
*Incorporated:* 12 July 2010  *Employees:* 18
*Net Worth:* £8,896,979  *Total Assets:* £10,070,034
*Registered Office:* The Office, Wield Yard, Lower Wield, Alresford, Hants, SO24 9RX
*Parent:* Wield Wines Limited
*Officers:* Bruce Stuart Green [1960] Finance Director; Gareth Howard Maxwell [1981] Director; Emma Mary Rice [1974] Director; Alexander Benjamin Melland Robinson [1987] Director/Customer Service Manager; Nicola Jane Robinson [1956] Director/Ski Wear Retailer; William Simon Melland Robinson [1955] Director/Farmer & Wine Producer


**Heartland Wines Europe Limited**
*Incorporated:* 24 July 2003
*Registered Office:* 1 Pearlbrook Estate, Chorley New Road, Horwich, Bolton, Lancs, BL6 5PX
*Officers:* Nicholas John Keukenmeester, Secretary; Grantley Bill Tilbrook, Secretary; Nicholas John Keukenmeester [1972] Managing Director [Australian]; Grantley Bill Tilbrook [1950] Director/Chartered Accountant (Ret) [Australian]


**Henners Limited**
*Incorporated:* 20 September 2006
*Net Worth Deficit:* £251,057  *Total Assets:* £338,409
*Registered Office:* Boundary House, Cheadle Point, Cheadle, Cheshire, SK8 2GG
*Parent:* Araldica Castelvero S.C.A
*Officers:* Iain Davies, Secretary; Iain Robert Davies [1970] Director/Accountant; Michael Joseph Moriarty [1965] Director; Dennis Whiteley [1961] Director


**Heron Ventures Ltd**
*Incorporated:* 26 September 2018
*Registered Office:* Heron Farm, Weston, Honiton, Devon, EX14 3NZ
*Shareholders:* Christine Sarah Helliwell; Peter John Helliwell
*Officers:* Dr Christine Sarah Helliwell [1980] Director/Business Executive; Peter John Helliwell [1979] Director/Business Executive


**James Herrick Wines Limited**
*Incorporated:* 23 August 1999
*Registered Office:* 9th Floor, Regal House, 70 London Road, Twickenham, Middlesex, TW1 3QS
*Officers:* Michelle Elizabeth Brampton [1972] Finance Director; Richard John Renwick [1969] Director/Chief Financial Officer Europe


**Highbrook Wine Estate Limited**
*Incorporated:* 22 February 2019
*Registered Office:* Hammingden Place, Hammingden Lane, Ardingly, Haywards Heath, W Sussex, RH17 6SR
*Shareholders:* Nigel Grenville Williams; Veronica Mary Williams
*Officers:* Dr Nigel Grenville Williams [1964] Director; Veronica Mary Williams [1966] Director

**Itasca Wines Limited**
*Incorporated:* 22 January 2018
*Registered Office:* Studio 5, The Old Kiln, Penncroft Farm, Itchel Lane, Crondall, Hants, GU10 5PX
*Shareholders:* Simon Porter; Malcolm Thomas Walker
*Officers:* Simon Porter [1959] Director/Farmer; Malcolm Thomas Walker [1958] Director/Film Producer

**K1 Beer PLC**
*Incorporated:* 10 July 2012
*Net Worth Deficit:* £245,872  *Total Assets:* £12,046
*Registered Office:* Building 3, Chiswick Park, 566 Chiswick High Road, London, W4 5YA
*Major Shareholder:* Keyvan Foroshani
*Officers:* Keyvan Foroshani [1963] Director/Chief Executive

**Karmely Limited**
*Incorporated:* 20 July 2015
*Registered Office:* Suite 14c, Link 665 Business Centre, Todd Hall Road, Haslingden, Rossendale, Lancs, BB4 5HU
*Officers:* Alexander Lorinkov, Secretary; Alexander Lorinkov [1967] Director/Trading [Bulgarian]

**Kidmore Vineyard Ltd**
*Incorporated:* 13 February 2018
*Registered Office:* Kidmore House, Chalkhouse Green Road, Kidmore End, Reading, Berks, RG4 9AR
*Shareholders:* Stephen Kendall; Niamh Kendall
*Officers:* Niamh Kendall [1972] Director/Horticulturist; Stephen Kendall [1965] Director/Wine Maker

**Kingscote Investments Limited**
*Incorporated:* 21 February 2017  *Employees:* 6
*Net Worth Deficit:* £193,083  *Total Assets:* £4,822,644
*Registered Office:* Kingscote Vineyards, Mill Place Farm, Vowels Lane, East Grinstead, W Sussex, RH19 4LG
*Major Shareholder:* Mark Dixon
*Officers:* Rudolf John Gabriel Lobo [1956] Director/Various Consultancy Roles at CXO Regus PLC; Paul Richard Smith [1981] Finance Director

**Kingscote Winery Ltd**
*Incorporated:* 6 July 2011
*Net Worth Deficit:* £10,718  *Total Assets:* £32,213
*Registered Office:* Pippens, Tickerage Lane, Blackboys, Uckfield, E Sussex, TN22 5LT
*Shareholder:* Anthony James Budd
*Officers:* Anthony James Budd [1968] Director; Christen Andrew Monge [1954] Director

**Kingsthorne Limited**
*Incorporated:* 7 February 2018
*Registered Office:* Sanctus House, The Waterfront, Stonehouse Park, Stonehouse, Glos, GL10 3UT
*Parent:* Sanctus Group Holdings Limited
*Officers:* Peter Alexander Cooke [1964] Director/Developer

**Kingwood Estate Limited**
*Incorporated:* 17 February 2016
*Registered Office:* Wyfold Meadows Farm, Wyfold, Reading, Berks, RG4 9HY
*Major Shareholder:* Ian Terence Smith
*Officers:* Ian Terence Smith [1978] Director

**KMSFish One Limited**
*Incorporated:* 8 January 2019
*Registered Office:* 5 Maveen Grove, Stockport, Cheshire, SK2 7BJ
*Major Shareholder:* Kang Ding
*Officers:* Kang Ding [1965] Director/Engineer [Chinese]

**La Remonta Limited**
*Incorporated:* 28 September 2005
*Registered Office:* 6 Timbermill Way, London, SW4 6LY
*Officers:* Luciann Flynn, Secretary; David Charles Gleave [1956] Director/Wine Merchant

**Lakemercy Ltd**
*Incorporated:* 14 August 2018
*Registered Office:* 6a Lines Street, Morecambe, Lancs, LA4 5ES
*Major Shareholder:* Daniel Roberts
*Officers:* Daniel Roberts [1992] Director/Consultant

**Laneberg Wine Ltd**
*Incorporated:* 4 September 2017
*Registered Office:* 20 Kingsway Interchange, Eleventh Avenue, Team Valley Trading Estate, Gateshead, Tyne & Wear, NE11 0JY
*Shareholders:* Marie Elise Lane; Nicholas Anthony Lawrie Lane
*Officers:* Marie Elise Lane [1980] Managing Director

**Langham Wine Limited**
*Incorporated:* 21 December 2011  *Employees:* 4
*Net Worth:* £275,494  *Total Assets:* £503,274
*Registered Office:* Bingham's Melcombe, Dorchester, DT2 7PZ
*Officers:* Alan Douglas Deves, Secretary; Alan Douglas Deves [1962] Director/Chartered Accountant; Daniel Ham [1985] Director; John Christopher Langham [1951] Director/Engineer; Justin Morley Langham [1963] Director/Farmer

**Victor Lanson Limited**
*Incorporated:* 14 April 1999
*Registered Office:* 5 Henchley Dene, Merrow Common, Guildford, Surrey, GU4 7BH
*Major Shareholder:* Victor Barbara Lanson
*Officers:* Susan Elaine Lanson, Secretary; Jean Victor Lanson [1966] Director/Wine Importer [French]

**Lanson UK Limited**
*Incorporated:* 7 June 1999
*Registered Office:* 5 Henchley Dene, Guildford, Surrey, GU4 7BH
*Shareholder:* Victor Barbara Lanson
*Officers:* Susan Elaine Lanson, Secretary; Jean Victor Lanson [1966] Director/Wine Importer [French]

**Laurel Vines, Vineyard & Winery Limited**
*Incorporated:* 13 August 2013
*Registered Office:* Laurel Farm, Aike, Driffield, E Yorks, YO25 9BG
*Shareholders:* Ian Leslie Sargent; Ann Sargent
*Officers:* Ann Sargent [1969] Director; Ian Leslie Sargent [1964] Director

**Leskaroon Falls Wine Estate Ltd**
*Incorporated:* 28 September 2017
*Registered Office:* Hawthorns, The Street, Effingham, Leatherhead, Surrey, KT24 5LQ
*Major Shareholder:* Leon Keith Sharples
*Officers:* Dr Leon Keith Sharples [1933] Director

**Lindisfarne Limited**
*Incorporated:* 3 June 1975  *Employees:* 18
*Net Worth:* £240,502  *Total Assets:* £811,398
*Registered Office:* St Aidan's Winery, Holy Island, Northumberland, TD15 2RX
*Parent:* Harry Hotspur Holdings Limited
*Officers:* Keith Caville Stephenson, Secretary; Ian Booth Robinson [1947] Director; Keith Caville Stephenson [1954] Director; Ronald Thomas Tait [1953] Director/Pottery Manager; Christopher Darryl Walwyn-James [1952] Director

**Lines Brew Co Ltd**
*Incorporated:* 16 May 2016  *Employees:* 3
*Net Worth:* £8,518  *Total Assets:* £167,946
*Registered Office:* 37a Bridge Street, Usk, Monmouthshire, NP15 1BQ
*Major Shareholder:* Thomas George Newman
*Officers:* Amy Louisa Scarcella [1993] Director/Operations Manager

**Little Horse Wines Limited**
*Incorporated:* 9 October 2017
*Registered Office:* 65 Woodbridge Road, Guildford, Surrey, GU1 4RD
*Shareholders:* Justin Bache; Tara Lawrence
*Officers:* Justin Bache [1969] Director; Tara Lawrence [1969] Director

**London Cru Ltd**
*Incorporated:* 5 September 2012  *Employees:* 3
*Net Worth Deficit:* £871,257  *Total Assets:* £556,837
*Registered Office:* 21-27 Seagrave Road, Fulham, London, SW6 1RP
*Shareholders:* William Tomlinson; Clifford John Roberson; Clifford John Roberson
*Officers:* Clifford John Roberson [1940] Director/Wine Merchant

**Ludlow Vineyard Limited**
*Incorporated:* 17 November 2003
*Registered Office:* Wainbridge House, Clee St Margaret, Craven Arms, Salop, SY7 9DT
*Shareholders:* Barbara Eileen Hardingham; Barbara Eileen Hardingham; Michael John Hardingham
*Officers:* Michael John Hardingham, Secretary/Administrator; Barbara Eileen Hardingham [1939] Director/Administrator; Michael John Hardingham [1956] Director/Administrator

**Luminati Wine Limited**
*Incorporated:* 21 March 2018
*Registered Office:* 221B Nantwich Road, Crewe, Cheshire, CW2 6DA
*Major Shareholder:* Lucifer Fawcett
*Officers:* Lucifer Fawcett [1989] Director

**Luxbev Limited**
*Incorporated:* 4 October 2017
*Registered Office:* 71-75 Shelton Street, Covent Garden, London, WC2H 9JQ
*Major Shareholder:* Hernando Ramirez
*Officers:* Hernando Ramirez, Secretary; Hernando Ramirez [1969] Director [French]

**Magnus Wines Ltd**
*Incorporated:* 4 May 2018
*Registered Office:* 45 Horsford Road, London, SW2 5BP
*Officers:* Duncan McCredie [1980] Director/Banker

**Marmoreccia Limited**
*Incorporated:* 2 March 2004
*Registered Office:* 6 Timbermill Way, London, SW4 6LY
*Major Shareholder:* Alberto Antonini
*Officers:* Luciann Flynn, Secretary; Alberto Antonini [1959] Director/Winemaker [Italian]

**Maskstice Ltd**
*Incorporated:* 23 July 2018
*Registered Office:* Unit 3 Trinity Centre, Park Farm Industrial Estate, Wellingborough, Northants, NN8 6ZB
*Major Shareholder:* Rebecca Spencer
*Officers:* Rowena Andres [1963] Director [Filipino]

**Mastropasqua & Brothers Ltd.**
*Incorporated:* 6 May 2016
*Registered Office:* c/o Sabino Antonio Mastrapasqua, 26 Baberton Mains Brae, Edinburgh, EH14 3HH
*Major Shareholder:* Sabino Antonio Mastrapasqua
*Officers:* Sabino Antonio Mastrapasqua [1973] Director [Italian]

**Maud Heath Wine Trading Limited**
*Incorporated:* 23 October 2007
*Net Worth Deficit:* £29,898  *Total Assets:* £264,597
*Registered Office:* Wick Bridge Farm, Wick Hill, Bremhill, Calne, Wilts, SN11 9LQ
*Parent:* The Garden Edge Farm Ltd
*Officers:* Elizabeth Bateman, Secretary; Dominic Thomas Oliver Bateman [1979] Director/Vineyard Management Executive; Elizabeth Bateman [1954] Director; Michael William Bateman [1946] Director

**Mayfield Vineyards Ltd**
*Incorporated:* 7 March 2014
*Registered Office:* 8 High Street, Heathfield, E Sussex, TN21 8LS
*Shareholders:* Jonica Mary Mandeville Fox; Gerard Ian Fox
*Officers:* Gerard Ian Fox [1964] Director/Banker; Jonica Mary Mandeville Fox [1958] Director/Wine Producer

**Alistair McCoist & Jeff East (Vintners) Ltd**
*Incorporated:* 28 March 2018
*Registered Office:* 12 Royal Crescent, Glasgow, G3 7SL
*Shareholders:* Alistair Murdoch McCoist; Jeffrey P M East
*Officers:* Jeffrey PM East [1968] Director; Alistair Murdoch McCoist [1962] Director

**Medland Manor Vineyard Ltd.**
*Incorporated:* 15 October 2018
*Registered Office:* Medland Manor, Cheriton Bishop, Exeter, EX6 6HE
*Major Shareholder:* Einar Finn Hafstad
*Officers:* Einar Finn Hafstad [1959] Managing Director

**Mereworth Wines Limited**
*Incorporated:* 2 March 2016
*Net Worth Deficit:* £91,036  *Total Assets:* £123,638
*Registered Office:* Suite 5, 10 Churchill Square, West Malling, Kent, ME19 4YU
*Major Shareholder:* Evelyn George William Boscawen
*Officers:* Evelyn George William Boscawen [1979] Director

**Mersea Island Brewery & Vineyard Ltd**
*Incorporated:* 22 May 2018
*Registered Office:* Mersea Vineyard, Rewsalls Lane, East Mersea, Colchester, Essex, CO5 8SX
*Shareholders:* Charlotte Barber; Mark Barber
*Officers:* Charlotte Barber [1987] Director; Jacqueline Barber [1951] Director; Mark Barber [1977] Director; Roger George William Barber [1949] Director

**Montgomery Vineyard Limited**
*Incorporated:* 4 August 2014
*Net Worth:* £1  *Total Assets:* £1
*Registered Office:* Cross Chambers, 9 High Street, Newtown, Powys, SY16 2NY
*Major Shareholder:* Tomas Woody Lennard
*Officers:* Tomas Woody Lennard [1979] Director

**Mosrowes Ltd**
*Incorporated:* 24 July 2018
*Registered Office:* Ground Floor Office, 108 Fore Street, Hertford, SG14 1AB
*Major Shareholder:* Frederick Haslam
*Officers:* Russiene Gile [1992] Director [Filipino]

**The New Zealand Wine Club Limited**
*Incorporated:* 12 July 1990
*Registered Office:* 9th Floor, Regal House, 70 London Road, Twickenham, Middlesex, TW1 3QS
*Parent:* Cellarmaster Wines Holdings (UK) Limited
*Officers:* Michelle Elizabeth Brampton [1972] Director/Financial Controller; Richard John Renwick [1969] Director/Chief Financial Officer Europe

**Nimblusher Ltd**
*Incorporated:* 23 July 2018
*Registered Office:* 214a Kettering Road, Northampton, NN1 4BN
*Shareholders:* Anthony Saflor; Robert Ashcroft
*Officers:* Anthony Saflor [1979] Director [Filipino]

**Noahs Estate Ltd**
*Incorporated:* 8 March 2018
*Registered Office:* 36 Park Lane, Wilberfoss, York, YO41 5PW
*Major Shareholder:* Jonathan Atkin
*Officers:* Jonathan Atkin [1984] Director/Businessman

**Nuclearbest Ltd**
*Incorporated:* 27 April 2018
*Registered Office:* 129 Burnley Road, Padiham, Burnley, Lancs, BB12 8BA
*Shareholders:* Ethel Joy Parulan; Chelsea Pollock
*Officers:* Ethel Joy Parulan [1985] Director [Filipino]

**Nutbourne Vineyards Limited**
*Incorporated:* 27 June 2005  *Employees:* 3
*Net Worth:* £370,245  *Total Assets:* £479,222
*Registered Office:* Nutbourne Manor, The Street, Nutbourne, Pulborough, W Sussex, RH20 2HE
*Major Shareholder:* Peter Alexis Gladwin
*Officers:* Bridget Gladwin, Secretary; Bridget Gladwin [1952] Director; Peter Alexis Gladwin [1954] Director

**Nyetimber (International Operations) Limited**
*Incorporated:* 28 April 2017
*Registered Office:* Nyetimber Vineyard, Gay Street, West Chiltington, W Sussex, RH20 2HH
*Major Shareholder:* Eric Niels Heerema
*Officers:* Robert Andrew MacDonald Watson, Secretary; Eric Niels Heerema [1960] Director [Dutch]

**Nyetimber Limited**
*Incorporated:* 15 July 2005
*Net Worth Deficit:* £29,259,980  *Total Assets:* £19,428,544
*Registered Office:* Nyetimber Vineyard, Gay Street, West Chiltington, W Sussex, RH20 2HH
*Parent:* Nyetimber Wines Limited
*Officers:* Robert Andrew MacDonald Watson, Secretary; Eric Niels Heerema [1960] Director [Dutch]

**Oastbrook Estates Limited**
*Incorporated:* 8 November 2017
*Registered Office:* Park Farm Oast, Junction Road, Bodiam, Robertsbridge, E Sussex, TN32 5XA
*Major Shareholder:* America Rodrigues Ribeiro Brewer
*Officers:* America Rodrigues Ribeiro Brewer, Secretary; America Rodrigues Ribeiro Brewer [1968] Director/Viticulture [Brazilian]; Nicholas Robert Brewer [1967] Director/Commodities

**Oeno Group Ltd**
*Incorporated:* 25 February 2019
*Registered Office:* Kemp House, 160 City Road, London, EC1V 2NX
*Shareholders:* Michael Doerr; Daniel Walker; Daniel Carnio
*Officers:* Daniel Walker [1985] Director/Company Owner

**Off The Line Limited**
*Incorporated:* 2 March 2016
*Registered Office:* Off The Line Vineyard, North Street, Hellingly, E Sussex, BN27 4EA
*Shareholders:* Ann-Marie Tynan; Kristina Mary Studzinski
*Officers:* Kristina Mary Studzinski [1964] Director; Ann-Marie Tynan [1965] Director [Irish]

**Oui Vino Limited**
*Incorporated:* 9 October 2018
*Registered Office:* 43 Polmor Road, Crowlas, Penzance, Cornwall, TR20 8DW
*Shareholder:* Hamish William Ludbrook
*Officers:* Hamish William Ludbrook [1983] Managing Director [New Zealander]

**Our Fathers Wines Ltd**
*Incorporated:* 13 January 2014
*Net Worth:* £2,935  *Total Assets:* £14,333
*Registered Office:* 7 Coltbridge Terrace, Edinburgh, EH12 6AB
*Major Shareholder:* Giles Cooke
*Officers:* Giles Cooke [1971] Director

**Penselwood Partnership Ltd**
*Incorporated:* 31 May 2018
*Registered Office:* Pen Mill Farm Cottage, Coombe Street, Penselwood, Wincanton, Somerset, BA9 8NF
*Shareholders:* Henry Strachey; Susan Strachey; Paul Trimming
*Officers:* Henry Strachey [1947] Director/Wine Merchant; Susan Strachey [1947] Director/Garden Centre Assistant; Paul Trimming [1961] Director/Wine Consultant

**Pharos AC Ltd.**
*Incorporated:* 27 May 2015  *Employees:* 2
*Previous:* Pharos HR Solutions Ltd.
*Net Worth:* £114,074  *Total Assets:* £188,151
*Registered Office:* 14 Cloisters Court, The Cloisters, Rickmansworth, Herts, WD3 1FE
*Shareholders:* Julie Jones; Mario Jose Moreno Garcia-Campero
*Officers:* Julie Jones [1966] Director/HR Consultant; Mario Jose Moreno Garcia-Campero [1971] Director [Spanish]

**Piersons Spirit of Wine Consulting Ltd**
*Incorporated:* 20 February 2014
*Net Worth Deficit:* £2,031  *Total Assets:* £68,262
*Registered Office:* c/o Approved Accounting Ltd, 36 Fifth Avenue, Havant, Hants, PO9 2PL
*Major Shareholder:* Didier Pierson
*Officers:* Didier Pierson [1966] Director [French]

**Pinglestone Estate Limited**
*Incorporated:* 15 December 2016
*Net Worth Deficit:* £60,872  *Total Assets:* £2,147,771
*Registered Office:* 1st Floor, 128 Buckingham Palace Road, London, SW1W 9SA
*Major Shareholder:* Paul-Francois Edouard Joseph Vranken
*Officers:* Clement Albert Pierlot [1980] Director/General Manager [French]; Gaylord Carlos Aurelien Sequeira [1985] Operations Director [French]; Paul-Francois Edouard Joseph Vranken [1947] Director/Chairman [French]

**Plummerden Estates Limited**
*Incorporated:* 11 December 2013
*Net Worth:* £15,353  *Total Assets:* £324,842
*Registered Office:* Suite 2.8, Monument House, 215 Marsh Road, Pinner, Middlesex, HA5 5NE
*Officers:* Barry Boon Shek Tay [1945] Director; Joyce Guat Kheng Tay [1953] Director

**Plummerden Lane Vineyards Limited**
*Incorporated:* 6 August 2013
*Net Worth Deficit:* £65,140  *Total Assets:* £323,087
*Registered Office:* Suite 2.8, Monument House, 215 Marsh Road, Pinner, Middlesex, HA5 5NE
*Shareholders:* Barry Boon Shek Tay; Joyce Guat Kheng Tay
*Officers:* Barry Boon Shek Tay [1945] Director/Scientist/Business Owner; Joyce Guat Kheng Tay [1953] Director/Financial Consultant

**Podere Delle Rune Ltd**
*Incorporated:* 4 July 2018
*Registered Office:* Maple House, The Street, Kettleburgh, Woodbridge, Suffolk, IP13 7JZ
*Shareholders:* Benjamin Charles Carr; Babila Gipponi
*Officers:* Benjamin Charles Carr [1991] Director

**Polgoon Vineyard Ltd**
*Incorporated:* 26 November 2018
*Registered Office:* Polgoon Farmhouse, Polgoon Farm, Rosehill, Penzance, Cornwall, TR20 8TE
*Shareholders:* John Paul Coulson; Kim Marie Coulson
*Officers:* John Paul Coulson [1962] Director/Winemaker

**Polmassick Vineyard Limited**
*Incorporated:* 24 May 2013
*Net Worth Deficit:* £66,196  *Total Assets:* £16,259
*Registered Office:* 22 Victoria Road, St Austell, Cornwall, PL25 4QD
*Shareholders:* Nicholas William West; Jo-Ann West
*Officers:* Jo-Ann West [1966] Director; Nicholas William West [1963] Director

**Port O' Bristol Ltd**
*Incorporated:* 4 June 2015
*Registered Office:* 34 Maple Road, Bristol, BS7 8RQ
*Shareholders:* Lela McTernan Mann; Anthony Michael Mann
*Officers:* Anthony Mann [1963] Director; Lela McTernan Mann [1964] Director

**Poulton Hill Estate Limited**
*Incorporated:* 29 November 2011  *Employees:* 2
*Net Worth Deficit:* £271,358  *Total Assets:* £237,358
*Registered Office:* Summer Lake, Spine Road East, South Cerney, Cirencester, Glos, GL7 5LW
*Major Shareholder:* Maxwell Hugh Thomas
*Officers:* Maxwell Hugh Thomas [1945] Director

**Premia Wines Ltd.**
*Incorporated:* 23 April 2014
*Net Worth Deficit:* £41,781  *Total Assets:* £19,429
*Registered Office:* 45 Egremont Drive, Lower Earley, Reading, Berks, RG6 3BS
*Major Shareholder:* Prem Jolly
*Officers:* Prem Jolly [1965] Director/Manager

**Press Shed Wines Limited**
*Incorporated:* 10 September 2018
*Registered Office:* 118 Netherhampton Road, Salisbury, Wilts, SP2 8LZ
*Major Shareholder:* Daniel Nicholas Ham
*Officers:* Daniel Nicholas Ham [1985] Director/Winemaker; Dr Nicola Anne Ham [1983] Director/Senior Technical Advisor

**The Pure Winery Limited**
*Incorporated:* 16 July 2018
*Registered Office:* Oakfield, 115 Station Road, Wootton, Ryde, Isle of Wight, PO33 4RG
*Major Shareholder:* Paul Anthony Gidley
*Officers:* Miriam Anna Horstman, Secretary; Adam Davis [1967] Commercial Director [Australian]; Paul Anthony Gidley [1968] Director; Johan Willem Maarten Jansen [1958] Director/Chief Executive Officer [Dutch]; Colin Bryan Rushmere [1962] Director/Chief Financial Officer [British/South African]

**Qualpro Greece Ltd.**
*Incorporated:* 7 January 2013
*Previous:* Qualcom Greece Ltd.
*Registered Office:* Kemp House, 160 City Road, London, EC1V 2NX
*Major Shareholder:* Antonios Stroumpoulis
*Officers:* Antonios Stroumpoulis [1983] Director/Electrical Engineer [Greek]

**Realsa Wines Import & Export Ltd**
*Incorporated:* 19 December 2014
*Net Worth Deficit:* £22,642  *Total Assets:* £58
*Registered Office:* No 1 Finns Farm, Smalls Hill Road, Norwood Hill, Horley, Surrey, RH6 0HR
*Officers:* Zack Kutty [1979] Director/Trading; Shinoj Vasudevan [1975] Director

**Rebel Pi Limited**
*Incorporated:* 21 August 2018
*Registered Office:* 1st Floor, 50 High Street, Cosham, Portsmouth, PO6 3AG
*Major Shareholder:* Jacquelyn Fast
*Officers:* Jacquelyn Fast [1983] Managing Director [Canadian]

**Ridgeview Estate Winery Limited**
*Incorporated:* 31 July 1995  *Employees:* 27
*Net Worth:* £2,214,557  *Total Assets:* £6,271,342
*Registered Office:* Upper Furzefield, Fragbarrow Lane, Ditchling Common, E Sussex, BN6 8TP
*Shareholders:* Tamara Jane Roberts; Simon Matthew Roberts; Graham Anthony Gayler; Christine Pamela Roberts
*Officers:* Tamara Roberts, Secretary; Graham Anthony Gayler [1958] Director; Christine Pamela Roberts [1944] Director; Simon Matthew Roberts [1971] Director/Winemaker; Tamara Roberts [1972] Director/Chief Executive; Arie Tukker [1950] Director [Dutch]

**Ridgeview Winery Contracts Limited**
*Incorporated:* 8 August 2001
*Registered Office:* Upper Furzefield, Fragbarrow Lane, Ditchling Common, Hassocks, W Sussex, BN6 8TP
*Parent:* Ridgeview Estate Winery Limited
*Officers:* Tamara Roberts, Secretary; Christine Pamela Roberts [1944] Director; Tamara Jane Roberts [1972] Director

**River Valley Vineyards Limited**
*Incorporated:* 24 July 2018
*Registered Office:* Sudbury Stables, Sudbury Road, Downham, Billericay, Essex, CM11 1LB
*Officers:* Stuart Pankhurst, Secretary; Chloe Pankhurst [1985] Director; Stuart Pankhurst [1975] Director

**Robert Roberts (NI) Limited**
*Incorporated:* 2 October 2002  *Employees:* 31
*Net Worth Deficit:* £3,630,192  *Total Assets:* £8,779,544
*Registered Office:* 138 University Street, Belfast, BT7 1HJ
*Parent:* Valeo Foods UK Limited
*Officers:* Brendan Feeney [1972] Director [Irish]; Seamus Kearney [1964] Director [Irish]

### Rockfield Wines Limited
*Incorporated:* 25 February 2016  *Employees:* 1
*Net Worth:* £190  *Total Assets:* £10,713
*Registered Office:* c/o Daud Qadri & Co, Global House, 303 Ballards Lane, London, N12 8NP
*Major Shareholder:* James Grey
*Officers:* James Grey [1978] Director/Wine Distributor

### Rose Wine Ltd.
*Incorporated:* 7 July 2009
*Net Worth Deficit:* £45,398  *Total Assets:* £6,958
*Registered Office:* Suite 11/1, 98 Lancefield Quay, Glasgow, G3 8JN
*Major Shareholder:* William McLean Burke
*Officers:* William McLean Burke [1947] Director

### Rosemary Vineyard Ltd.
*Incorporated:* 27 September 2011  *Employees:* 14
*Net Worth:* £69,197  *Total Assets:* £143,479
*Registered Office:* Rosemary Vineyard, Smallbrook Lane, Ryde, Isle of Wight, PO33 4BE
*Major Shareholder:* Conrad Gauntlett
*Officers:* Conrad Martin Gauntlett [1953] Director/Businessman

### Ross Earl Wine Co., Ltd.
*Incorporated:* 21 August 2018
*Registered Office:* Chase Business Centre, 39-41 Chase Side, London, N14 5BP
*Shareholders:* Hongxiao Wang; Xuefeng Wang; Dianbo Zhao
*Officers:* Hongxiao Wang [1973] Director [Chinese]

### Rothley Wine Limited
*Incorporated:* 25 February 2014
*Net Worth Deficit:* £62,990  *Total Assets:* £41,712
*Registered Office:* 154 Rothley Road, Mountsorrel, Leics, LE12 7JX
*Major Shareholder:* Sarah Elizabeth Evans Robson
*Officers:* Sarah Elizabeth Evans Robson [1956] Director/Principal Lecturer

### Rudd Farms Limited
*Incorporated:* 11 November 2015  *Employees:* 8
*Net Worth Deficit:* £465,117  *Total Assets:* £2,364,268
*Registered Office:* Wells House, Stephenson's Way, The Wyvern Business Park, Derby, DE21 6LY
*Parent:* Rother House Finance Limited
*Officers:* Anne Margaret Hawley, Secretary; Timothy Nigel Rudd [1971] Director

### San Gregorio UK Limited
*Incorporated:* 20 January 2016
*Registered Office:* 1st Floor, 163 Eversholt Street, London, NW1 1BU
*Parent:* Casual Dining Limited
*Officers:* Giles Matthew Oliver David, Secretary; Giles Matthew Oliver David [1967] Director/Accountant; Stephen Richards [1967] Director

### Sant' Elia Limited
*Incorporated:* 19 November 2013
*Net Worth Deficit:* £7,047  *Total Assets:* £100
*Registered Office:* 3a Bellmere Gardens, Malvern, Worcs, WR14 3HE
*Shareholders:* Jerry Philip Avis; Irene Elizabeth Avis
*Officers:* Jerry Avis, Secretary; Irene Avis [1950] Director; Jerry Philip Avis [1946] Director

### Santa Rita Europe Limited
*Incorporated:* 18 July 2003  *Employees:* 6
*Net Worth:* £823,252  *Total Assets:* £980,211
*Registered Office:* Cranbrook House, 287-291 Banbury Road, Summertown, Oxford, OX2 7JQ
*Parent:* Vina Santa Rita SA
*Officers:* Jose Miguel Benavente, Secretary; Jose Miguel Benavente [1977] Director [Chilean]; Jaime de La Barra [1981] Director [Chilean]; Andres Lavados [1972] Director [Chilean]

### Sapphiremimic Ltd
*Incorporated:* 20 August 2018
*Registered Office:* 97 Whittle Street, Worsley, Manchester, M28 3WY
*Major Shareholder:* Michelle Barlow
*Officers:* Michelle Barlow [1982] Director/Consultant

### Schoenlaub Limited
*Incorporated:* 20 November 2018
*Registered Office:* 7-9 Ferdinand Street, London, NW1 8ES
*Major Shareholder:* Thomas Schonlaub
*Officers:* Thomas Schonlaub [1974] Managing Director [German]

### Selectia Wine Ltd
*Incorporated:* 4 October 2018
*Registered Office:* 20 Campden Green, Solihull, W Midlands, B92 8HG
*Major Shareholder:* Jose Ignacio Clavijo Barrio
*Officers:* Jose Ignacio Clavijo Barrio [1968] Commercial Director [Spanish]; Francisca Isabel Marquez [1969] Director/Manager [Spanish]

### Sharpham Partnership Limited
*Incorporated:* 1 April 1992  *Employees:* 26
*Net Worth:* £918,296  *Total Assets:* £1,427,812
*Registered Office:* Sharpham House, Ashprington, Totnes, Devon, TQ9 7UT
*Major Shareholder:* Mark Richard William Sharman
*Officers:* Mark Richard William Sharman, Secretary; Mark Richard William Sharman [1959] Director/Manager

### Sharpham Wine Limited
*Incorporated:* 14 January 2019
*Registered Office:* Owl's Roost, Beenleigh, Harbertonford, Totnes, Devon, TQ9 7EF
*Major Shareholder:* Mark Richard William Sharman
*Officers:* Mark Richard William Sharman [1959] Director/Winemaker

### Shawsgate Limited
*Incorporated:* 28 January 1999  *Employees:* 7
*Net Worth:* £20,387  *Total Assets:* £433,487
*Registered Office:* Buces Farm, Mendlesham, Suffolk, IP14 5NR
*Officers:* Leslie Jarrett [1952] Director

### Sibling Winery Limited
*Incorporated:* 19 September 2018
*Registered Office:* 3 Hill Top, Loxley, Warwick, CV35 9JU
*Officers:* Laura Marie Mitchell, Secretary; Rosanna Laura Mitchell [1990] Director; Daniel Keith Smith [1969] Director; Patrick James Smith [1969] Director

### Silva and Cosens Limited
*Incorporated:* 3 April 1914  *Employees:* 3
*Net Worth:* £47,086,000  *Total Assets:* £47,200,000
*Registered Office:* 7-8 Great James Street, London, WC1N 3DF
*Parent:* Silva & Cosens Holdings Limited
*Officers:* Paul Nunnerley Hall, Secretary; John Andrew Douglas Symington [1960] Director/Port Shipper; Paul Douglas Symington [1953] Director; Rupert Alexander Douglas Symington [1964] Director/Wine Merchant

**Silverton Wines Ltd**
*Incorporated:* 25 October 2017
*Registered Office:* Redwoods, 2 Clyst Works, Clyst Road, Topsham, Exeter, Devon, EX3 0DB
*Major Shareholder:* Ivan James Jordan
*Officers:* Janice James [1966] Director/Market Gardener [Irish]; Ivan James Jordan [1973] Director/Architect [Irish]

**Simpsons Wine Estate Limited**
*Incorporated:* 9 October 2013 *Employees:* 6
*Net Worth:* £358,503 *Total Assets:* £2,802,821
*Registered Office:* c/o Turcan Connell, 12 Stanhope Gate, London, W1K 1AW
*Shareholders:* Charles William Simpson; Ruth Elizabeth Simpson
*Officers:* Charles William Simpson [1969] Director; Ruth Elizabeth Simpson [1971] Director

**Simpsons Wine Imports Limited**
*Incorporated:* 12 February 2002 *Employees:* 2
*Previous:* Serenity Wines Limited
*Net Worth Deficit:* £65,211 *Total Assets:* £11,098
*Registered Office:* Princes Exchange, 1 Earl Grey Street, Edinburgh, EH3 9EE
*Officers:* Ruth Elizabeth Simpson, Secretary; Charles William Simpson [1969] Director; Ruth Elizabeth Simpson [1971] Director

**Skinnybrands Ltd**
*Incorporated:* 2 September 2015 *Employees:* 3
*Net Worth:* £1,375,318 *Total Assets:* £1,702,059
*Registered Office:* Ashton Old Baths, Stamford Street West, Ashton under Lyne, Lancs, OL6 7FW
*Shareholders:* Thomas Neale Bell; Gary Nicholas Conway
*Officers:* Mihai Albu [1962] Director [Romanian]; Thomas Neale Bell [1989] Director/Alcohol Manufacturer; Gary Nicholas Conway [1971] Director [Irish]

**Skyblossom Ltd**
*Incorporated:* 24 May 2018
*Registered Office:* 129 Burnley Road, Padiham, Burnley, Lancs, BB12 8BA
*Major Shareholder:* George Taylor
*Officers:* Giselle Gadingan [1997] Director [Filipino]

**Sloegasm Limited**
*Incorporated:* 27 January 2009
*Registered Office:* One Dunston Court, Dunston Road, Chesterfield, Derbys, S41 8NL
*Officers:* Ashley Ryck Turner [1968] Director

**Somborne Valley Vineyard Limited**
*Incorporated:* 23 March 2001
*Net Worth Deficit:* £106,161 *Total Assets:* £125,200
*Registered Office:* Hoplands Estate, Kings Somborne, Stockbridge, Hants, SO20 6QH
*Shareholders:* Nigel Wolsenholme; Jacqueline Wolsenholme
*Officers:* Kenneth John Stratton, Secretary/Accountant; Vicki Alison Cook [1964] Director/Personal Assistant; Jacqueline Wolstenholme [1960] Director/Administrator; Nigel Timothy Wolstenholme [1956] Director/Surveyor

**Somerby Vineyards Limited**
*Incorporated:* 20 December 2006 *Employees:* 1
*Net Worth Deficit:* £709,240 *Total Assets:* £291,551
*Registered Office:* 1-3 Dudley Street, Grimsby, N E Lincs, DN31 2AW
*Shareholders:* William Hobson; Linda Hobson
*Officers:* Linda Hobson, Secretary; Linda Hobson [1950] Director/Secretary; William Hobson [1944] Director/Fish Merchant

**Somm in the Must Ltd**
*Incorporated:* 5 December 2017
*Registered Office:* Wework, 115 Mare Street, London, E8 4RU
*Shareholders:* Nicolas Pierron; Pierrick Gorrichon
*Officers:* Pierrick Gorrichon [1993] Director/Assistant Head Sommelier [French]; Nicolas Pierron [1982] Director/Head Sommelier [French]

**South East Vineyards Association Ltd**
*Incorporated:* 29 November 2012
*Net Worth:* £151 *Total Assets:* £1,201
*Registered Office:* Albury Vineyard Ltd, Shere Road, Albury, Guildford, Surrey, GU5 9BW
*Officers:* Alison Jane Englefield [1960] Director/Winemaker; Nicholas Edward Wenman [1956] Director

**South East Wineries Limited**
*Incorporated:* 28 September 2017
*Net Worth Deficit:* £21,622 *Total Assets:* £951,756
*Registered Office:* Kingscote Vineyards, Mill Place Farm, Vowels Lane, Kingscote, East Grinstead, W Sussex, RH19 4LG
*Parent:* Vineyard Holdings Ltd
*Officers:* Kieran Patrick Balmer [1976] Director; Sophie Emma Louise Balmer [1988] Director; Rudolf John Gabriel Lobo [1956] Director; Paul Richard Smith [1981] Finance Director

**Southcorp Wines Europe Limited**
*Incorporated:* 8 April 1993
*Registered Office:* 9th Floor, Regal House, 70 London Road, Twickenham, Middlesex, TW1 3QS
*Parent:* Treasury Wine Estates EMEA Limited
*Officers:* Michelle Elizabeth Brampton [1972] Finance Director; Richard John Renwick [1969] Director/Chief Financial Officer Europe

**Southern England Wines (UK) Ltd**
*Incorporated:* 22 March 2016 *Employees:* 3
*Net Worth:* £2,593,435 *Total Assets:* £2,754,968
*Registered Office:* Amelia House, Crescent Road, Worthing, W Sussex, BN11 1QR
*Shareholder:* John Richard Ball
*Officers:* John Richard Ball [1962] Director; Michael Norman Smith [1953] Director

**Spirits Development & Management Company (SDMC) Limited**
*Incorporated:* 16 December 2013
*Net Worth:* £631,395 *Total Assets:* £3,439,762
*Registered Office:* Citypoint, 65 Haymarket Terrace, Edinburgh, EH12 5HD
*Major Shareholder:* Michel Picard
*Officers:* Michel Bernard Picard [1942] Director [French]

**St Emilion Holdings Limited**
*Incorporated:* 10 April 2007
*Net Worth Deficit:* £23,871 *Total Assets:* £2,159,654
*Registered Office:* 18 Fitzhardinge Street, London, W1H 6EQ
*Shareholders:* Martin John Krajewski; Verite Trust Company Limited as Trustees of The Kiwi Trust
*Officers:* Martin John Krajewski, Secretary; Anil Dave [1955] Director/Chartered Accountant; Martin John Krajewski [1955] Director/Wine Maker; Marcus Andrew Le Grice [1965] Director/Banker

**Stangro Limited**
*Incorporated:* 10 December 1973
*Registered Office:* The Old Vicarage, Vicarage Lane, Nettleham, Lincoln, LN2 2RH
*Shareholder:* Raymond John Stanbridge
*Officers:* Dr Raymond John Stanbridge, Secretary; Paul John Stanbridge [1950] Director/Farmer; Dr Raymond John Stanbridge [1947] Director; Sidney John Stanbridge [1923] Director/Farmer

**Stanlake Park Company Limited**
*Incorporated:* 6 November 1978
*Net Worth Deficit:* £1,032,336  *Total Assets:* £619,355
*Registered Office:* Stanlake Park, Twyford, Berks, RG10 0BN
*Major Shareholder:* Daniel James Goss-Custard
*Officers:* Daniel James Goss-Custard [1973] Director

**Sticle Vineyard Ltd**
*Incorporated:* 28 February 2019
*Registered Office:* Sticle, Castle Road, Pencader, Carmarthenshire, SA39 9AN
*Shareholder:* Christiane Racine
*Officers:* Andrew Robert Barnes [1995] Sales Director; Cedric Racine [1997] Accounts Director [Canadian]; Christiane Racine [1962] Managing Director; Justin Racine [1993] Operations Director; LEA Racine [2001] Innovations Director; Vincent Racine [1996] IT Director [Canadian]

**The Stonor Valley Winery Limited**
*Incorporated:* 26 October 2012  *Employees:* 2
*Net Worth:* £3,043,077  *Total Assets:* £3,215,818
*Registered Office:* 9 Thorney Leys Park, Witney, Oxon, OX28 4GE
*Shareholders:* Stephen Patrick Duckett; Fiona Louise Duckett
*Officers:* Fiona Louise Duckett [1968] Director; Stephen Patrick Duckett [1967] Director

**Stopham Vineyard Ltd**
*Incorporated:* 13 February 2008  *Employees:* 3
*Net Worth:* £445,729  *Total Assets:* £536,835
*Registered Office:* Stopham Vineyard Winery, Stopham, Pulborough, W Sussex, RH20 1EE
*Shareholder:* Simon Martin Woodhead
*Officers:* Sir Peter Woodhead, Secretary; Simon Martin Woodhead [1966] Director/Winemaker

**Strawberry Bank Liqueurs Limited**
*Incorporated:* 30 May 2002  *Employees:* 2
*Net Worth Deficit:* £10,308  *Total Assets:* £23,585
*Registered Office:* Wood Yeat, Crosthwaite, Kendal, Cumbria, LA8 8HX
*Shareholder:* John Michael Walsh
*Officers:* John Michael Walsh, Secretary; John Michael Walsh [1943] Director/Brewer

**Strawberry Hill Vineyard Limited**
*Incorporated:* 2 December 2010  *Employees:* 1
*Net Worth:* £7,494  *Total Assets:* £37,428
*Registered Office:* Strawberry Hill Vineyard, Orchard Road, Newent, Glos, GL18 1DQ
*Major Shareholder:* Timothy Chance
*Officers:* Tim Chance, Secretary; Tim Chance [1952] Director

**Sugrue Pierre Limited**
*Incorporated:* 26 March 2013
*Net Worth:* £13,945  *Total Assets:* £130,505
*Registered Office:* Island Cottage, Rock Lane, Washington, Pulborough, W Sussex, RH20 3BL
*Major Shareholder:* Dermot Sugrue
*Officers:* Dermot Sugrue [1974] Director/Winemaker

**Sussex Vineyards Limited**
*Incorporated:* 3 November 2006
*Registered Office:* 8 High Street, Heathfield, E Sussex, TN21 8LS
*Major Shareholder:* Gerard Ian Fox
*Officers:* Jonica Mary Mandeville Fox, Secretary; Gerard Ian Fox [1964] Director/Banker

**Sutter Home Winery Limited**
*Incorporated:* 22 August 2002
*Registered Office:* 36-38 Westbourne Grove, Newton Road, London, W2 5SH
*Shareholders:* Louis Trinchero; Roger John Trinchero
*Officers:* Louis Trinchero [1936] Director/Winery Owner [American]; Roger John Trinchero [1946] Director/Winery Owner [American]

**Swift Half Collective Ltd**
*Incorporated:* 2 May 2017
*Registered Office:* Hamlet Cottage, St Michaels Church Road, Liverpool, L17 7BD
*Shareholder:* Conor Foley
*Officers:* Conor Foley [1985] Managing Director [Irish]; Peter Michael John Hunter [1987] Marketing & Sales Director; Danny McCay [1985] Artistic Director [Irish]

**T & P Weinbau**
*Incorporated:* 8 September 2016
*Registered Office:* The Picasso Building, Caldervale Road, Wakefield, W Yorks, WF1 5PF
*Officers:* Dieter Heinz Friedrich Kuester [1949] Director/Retiree [German]

**Taylor Family Wines Ltd.**
*Incorporated:* 4 December 2017
*Registered Office:* 9 Townsend Gate, Berkhamsted, Herts, HP4 2FZ
*Major Shareholder:* Alexander David Nicholas Taylor
*Officers:* Alexander David Nicholas Taylor [1979] Director; Naomi Alexandra Taylor [1992] Director/Events Manager

**Tewaina Ltd**
*Incorporated:* 24 September 2018
*Registered Office:* 71-75 Shelton Street, Covent Garden, London, WC2H 9JQ
*Shareholders:* Victoria Khan; Andrey Li
*Officers:* Victoria Khan [1977] Director/Lawyer [Russian]

**Three Choirs Vineyards Limited**
*Incorporated:* 30 August 1984  *Employees:* 49
*Net Worth:* £1,459,179  *Total Assets:* £2,999,865
*Registered Office:* Baldwins Farm, Newent, Glos, GL18 1LS
*Shareholder:* Helena Oldacre
*Officers:* Thomas Richard Rogers Shaw, Secretary/Director; Martin Hoult Fowke [1962] Production Director; Katharine Helena Morley [1964] Director; Thomas Richard Rogers Shaw [1960] Director; Henry Bonner Shouler [1937] Director

**Tillingham Wines Limited**
*Incorporated:* 28 February 2017
*Net Worth Deficit:* £18,691  *Total Assets:* £189,541
*Registered Office:* Dew Farm, Church Lane, Peasmarsh, Rye, E Sussex, TN31 6XD
*Shareholders:* Benjamin James Walgate; Rt Hon Terence Viscount Devonport
*Officers:* Rt Hon Terence Viscount Devonport [1944] Director; Benjamin James Walgate [1979] Director

**Tinston Wines & Ciders Limited**
*Incorporated:* 2 October 2017
*Registered Office:* 24 Crayford Road, Brighton, BN2 4DQ
*Major Shareholder:* Liam Tinston
*Officers:* Liam Tinston [1984] Director/Winemaker

**Too Far North Wine Co Ltd**
*Incorporated:* 12 December 2017
*Registered Office:* 6 Grange Lane, Magherafelt, Co Derry, BT45 5EU
*Officers:* Brian Shaw [1987] Director/Winemaker [Irish]

**Torview Wines Limited**
*Incorporated:* 22 January 2009
*Net Worth Deficit:* £63,037  *Total Assets:* £51,298
*Registered Office:* Beara Farm, Sheepwash, Beaworthy, Devon, EX21 5PB
*Shareholders:* Berin James Locks Gowan; Timothy Gowan
*Officers:* Catriona Mary Gowan, Secretary; Catriona Mary Gowan [1975] Director; Timothy Gowan [1975] Director/Wine Producer

**Treasury Wine Estates EMEA Limited**
*Incorporated:* 26 September 1986  *Employees:* 113
*Net Worth:* £110,482,000  *Total Assets:* £205,760,000
*Registered Office:* Regal House, 70 London Road, Twickenham, Middlesex, TW1 3QS
*Officers:* Michelle Elizabeth Brampton [1972] Finance Director; Richard John Renwick [1969] Director/Chief Financial Officer Europe

**Treasury Wine Estates UK Brands Limited**
*Incorporated:* 25 February 2011
*Net Worth:* £92,093,024  *Total Assets:* £92,878,672
*Registered Office:* 9th Floor, Regal House, 70 London Road, Twickenham, Middlesex, TW1 3QS
*Parent:* FBL Holdings Limited
*Officers:* Michelle Elizabeth Brampton [1972] Finance Director; Richard John Renwick [1969] Director/Chief Financial Officer Europe

**Tremayne Food and Drink Limited**
*Incorporated:* 10 January 2019
*Registered Office:* The Old Nuclear Bunker, Pednavounder, Coverack, Cornwall, TR12 6SE
*Shareholders:* Mark Stephen Nattrass; Leonora Helen Nattrass
*Officers:* Dr Mark Stephen Nattrass [1966] Director

**TWE Finance (UK) Limited**
*Incorporated:* 31 January 2011
*Net Worth:* £3,446,432  *Total Assets:* £60,580,812
*Registered Office:* 9th Floor, Regal House, London Road, Twickenham, Middlesex, TW1 3QS
*Parent:* Treasury Wine Estates EMEA Limited
*Officers:* Michelle Elizabeth Brampton [1972] Finance Director; Richard John Renwick [1969] Director/Chief Financial Officer Europe

**UK Wine Services Limited**
*Incorporated:* 17 November 2016
*Net Worth:* £5,951  *Total Assets:* £84,626
*Registered Office:* Dew Farm, Dew Lane, Peasmarsh, Rye, E Sussex, TN31 6XD
*Major Shareholder:* Ben Walgate
*Officers:* Ben Walgate, Secretary; Ben Walgate [1979] Director/Winemaker

**United Manufacturing Europe Ltd**
*Incorporated:* 6 October 2000
*Registered Office:* 242 Kingsbury Road, London, NW9 0BG
*Major Shareholder:* Jairaj Jashanmal Dadlani
*Officers:* Jairaj Jashanmal Dadlani [1957] Director/Company Manager

**Universal Robo Innovations Limited**
*Incorporated:* 24 May 2018
*Registered Office:* 71-75 Shelton Street, London, WC2H 9JQ
*Officers:* Ankit Mehta [1981] Director [Indian]

**Uponcellar Ltd**
*Incorporated:* 4 June 2018
*Registered Office:* 2nd Floor, Clyde Offices, 48 West George Street, Glasgow, G2 1BP
*Major Shareholder:* Stephen McLoughlin
*Officers:* Dianne Jerica Lavalle [1988] Director [Filipino]

**Upperton Vineyards Limited**
*Incorporated:* 22 March 2016
*Net Worth Deficit:* £56,601  *Total Assets:* £983,512
*Registered Office:* Amelia House, Crescent Road, Worthing, W Sussex, BN11 1QR
*Shareholder:* John Richard Ball
*Officers:* John Richard Ball [1962] Director; Michael Norman Smith [1953] Director

**Urban Initiatives Limited**
*Incorporated:* 29 June 2016
*Net Worth Deficit:* £41,821  *Total Assets:* £89,136
*Registered Office:* 14b Graces Road, London, SE5 8PA
*Major Shareholder:* John Warwick Smith
*Officers:* John Warwick Smith [1980] Director/Investment Professional

**Vergecosse Limited**
*Incorporated:* 8 March 2006
*Net Worth:* £1,211,381  *Total Assets:* £1,211,981
*Registered Office:* Caledonian Exchange, 19a Canning Street, Edinburgh, EH3 8HE
*Officers:* Peter David Tweedie, Secretary; Neil Stuart Davidson [1959] Services Director; John Watson King [1954] Director; Richard Haydon Philips [1957] Director; Robert Anthony Reeves [1944] Director (2 Charities)

**The Verrillo Partnership Limited**
*Incorporated:* 1 March 2017
*Net Worth Deficit:* £46,046  *Total Assets:* £117,415
*Registered Office:* 168 Church Road, Hove, E Sussex, BN3 2DL
*Shareholders:* Sergio Milan Verrillo; Lynsey Abernethy Verrillo
*Officers:* Lynsey Abernethy Verrillo [1981] Director/Senior Manager; Sergio Milan Verrillo [1981] Director/Winemaker [Hungarian]

**Vesteraalen Vinproduksjon Limited**
*Incorporated:* 30 August 2017
*Registered Office:* Third Floor, 207 Regent Street, London, W1B 3HH
*Parent:* Vabene Agency Limited
*Officers:* Gerhard Kolflaath [1962] Director [Norwegian]

**Villa Maria New Zealand Wineries (UK) Limited**
*Incorporated:* 29 July 2015  *Employees:* 2
*Net Worth:* £22,400  *Total Assets:* £40,024
*Registered Office:* Herschel House, 58 Herschel Street, Slough, Berks, SL1 1PG
*Major Shareholder:* George Vjeceslav Fistonich
*Officers:* Sir George Vjeceslav Fistonich [1939] Director/Chief Executive Officer [New Zealander]; Karen Theresa Fistonich [1962] Director/Chairperson [New Zealander]; Fabian George Yakich [1955] Executive Director [New Zealander]

**Vine Revival UK Limited**
*Incorporated:* 29 March 2016
*Registered Office:* 21 Calais Street, London, SE5 9LP
*Major Shareholder:* Christelle Anita Guibert
*Officers:* Christelle Anita Guibert [1973] Director [French]

**The Vineyard Dynamics Co. Limited**
*Incorporated:* 1 December 2009
*Net Worth:* £755  *Total Assets:* £12,988
*Registered Office:* 39 Station Road, Liphook, Hants, GU30 7DW
*Shareholders:* James George Sacha; Andrew Charles Sacha
*Officers:* Andrew Charles Sacha [1957] Director/Consultant; James George Sacha [1986] Director/Sales Executive

**Viniage Wines Limited**
*Incorporated:* 3 September 2013
*Net Worth Deficit:* £80,052  *Total Assets:* £24,020
*Registered Office:* 38 Bathurst Mews, London, W2 2SB
*Shareholders:* David Andrew Joynt; Antoine Gilles Rene Marcel Acloque
*Officers:* Antoine Acloque [1987] Director [French]; David Andrew Joynt [1977] Director

**Vinus Wine Ltd**
*Incorporated:* 2 February 2018
*Registered Office:* Sterling House, High Street, Wellingborough, Northants, NN8 4HL
*Major Shareholder:* Sarah Louise Williams
*Officers:* Sarah Louise Williams [1979] Director

**Vitosha Wine Ltd**
*Incorporated:* 10 January 2019
*Registered Office:* 7 Victoria Road, Alton, Hants, GU34 2DH
*Shareholders:* Umesh Prasad; Neelesh Prasad
*Officers:* Umesh Prasad [1965] Director

**Walton Brook Vineyard Limited**
*Incorporated:* 20 August 2014
*Net Worth Deficit:* £1,720  *Total Assets:* £20,524
*Registered Office:* Horse Leys Farm, 147 Melton Road, Burton on the Wolds, Loughborough, Leics, LE12 5TQ
*Shareholders:* Trevor Eggleston; Ceri Griffiths
*Officers:* Trevor Eggleston [1943] Director/Farmer; Ceri Griffiths [1965] Director

**Weinhouse Limited**
*Incorporated:* 31 March 2014  *Employees:* 3
*Net Worth:* £104,480  *Total Assets:* £183,224
*Registered Office:* 50 Regent Street, Stoke on Trent, Staffs, ST4 5HG
*Major Shareholder:* Daniel John Canavan
*Officers:* Kathleen Miller, Secretary; Berendina Geertruida Canavan [1952] Director; Daniel John Canavan [1977] Director

**Welland Valley Vineyard Ltd**
*Incorporated:* 5 December 1985  *Employees:* 2
*Previous:* Lex Publishing Limited
*Net Worth Deficit:* £39,991  *Total Assets:* £22,171
*Registered Office:* Vine Lodge, Hothorpe Road, Marston Trussell, Market Harborough, Leics, LE16 9TX
*Shareholders:* David Stafford Bates; Angela Jane Primrose Bates
*Officers:* David Stafford Bates, Secretary; Angela Jane Primrose Bates [1944] Director/Publisher; David Stafford Bates [1942] Director/Solicitor Retired

**Westwell Wine Estates Ltd**
*Incorporated:* 6 June 2017
*Net Worth:* £2,066,125  *Total Assets:* £2,122,114
*Registered Office:* Fawcett House, Scugdale Road, Swainby, Northallerton, N Yorks, DL6 3DS
*Officers:* Adrian Pike [1971] Director; John Philip Henri Scarlett [1986] Director; Rosemary Anne Taylor [1954] Director; Simon Timothy Wren [1982] Director

**Weyborne Limited**
*Incorporated:* 6 April 2017
*Registered Office:* Finsgate, 5-7 Cranwood Street, London, EC1V 9EE
*Parent:* Salkeld Limited
*Officers:* Nicholas Antony Clarke [1961] Director

**Wild Life Botanicals Ltd**
*Incorporated:* 28 February 2019
*Registered Office:* 20-22 Wenlock Road, London, N1 7GU
*Major Shareholder:* Jonathan Paul Steadman Archer
*Officers:* Jonathan Paul Steadman Archer [1966] Director

**The Wine Fusion Innovations Limited**
*Incorporated:* 12 June 2009
*Registered Office:* The Clarence Centre, 6 St Georges Circus, London, SE1 6FE
*Shareholders:* The Wine Fusion Limited; Giles Edward Andreae
*Officers:* Giles Edward Andreae [1966] Director/Poet; John Michael Hope [1949] Director; Andrew George Porton [1974] Director/Sales & Marketing; Christopher Luke Smith [1969] Director

**The Wine Fusion Limited**
*Incorporated:* 14 January 2008  *Employees:* 4
*Net Worth Deficit:* £92,039  *Total Assets:* £1,592,013
*Registered Office:* Unit 2 Greencroft Estates, Tower Road, Annfield Plain, Stanley, Co Durham, DH9 7XP
*Parent:* Lanchester Wine Cellars Limited
*Officers:* Adam Richard Black [1968] Director; Anthony Austin Cleary [1952] Director; Veronica Anne Cleary [1954] Director; Andrew George Porton [1974] Director/Wine Merchant; Mark Anthony Satchwell [1964] Director

**Winebar Pouch Company Ltd**
*Incorporated:* 14 October 2013
*Net Worth Deficit:* £51,250  *Total Assets:* £11,996
*Registered Office:* Arch 7 Westgate Road, Newcastle upon Tyne, NE1 1SA
*Major Shareholder:* Mark John Hall
*Officers:* Mark John Hall [1961] Director

**Winehood Ltd**
*Incorporated:* 23 November 2018
*Registered Office:* 40b Napier Road, London, NW10 5XJ
*Shareholders:* Francesca Anna Darby; Emma Louise Alicia Collyear
*Officers:* Emma Louise Alicia Collyear [1985] Director/Co-Founder; Francesca Anna Darby [1990] Director/Co-Founder

**Wines of Douro Limited**
*Incorporated:* 12 June 2017
*Registered Office:* 1 Buttermere Close, Morden, Surrey, SM4 4SG
*Major Shareholder:* Helena Pinto
*Officers:* Helena Pinto [1983] Director [French]

**Witham Wines Limited**
*Incorporated:* 15 April 2016
*Net Worth Deficit:* £7,586  *Total Assets:* £10,691
*Registered Office:* Unit 4 Partnership House, Withambrook Park Industrial Estate, Grantham, Lincs, NG31 9ST
*Major Shareholder:* Gemma Ruigrok
*Officers:* Gemma Ruigrok, Secretary; Charles Ruigrok [1986] Director/Manufacture and Distribution of Wine; Gemma Ruigrok [1986] Director/Manufacture and Distribution of Wine

**Wolf Oak Limited**
*Incorporated:* 5 June 2013  *Employees:* 1
*Net Worth Deficit:* £39,299  *Total Assets:* £42,329
*Registered Office:* 40-42 High Street, Maldon, Essex, CM9 5PN
*Major Shareholder:* George Michel Klat
*Officers:* George Michel Klat [1975] Director

**Woodchester Valley Winery Limited**
*Incorporated:* 6 October 2014  *Employees:* 1
*Net Worth:* £895  *Total Assets:* £1,237,146
*Registered Office:* Smith House, George Street, Nailsworth, Stroud, Glos, GL6 0AG
*Shareholders:* Fiona Jane Shiner; Brendan Niall Shiner
*Officers:* Fiona Jane Shiner [1961] Director

**World Wine Investors UK Limited**
*Incorporated:* 10 September 2012  *Employees:* 8
*Net Worth:* £11,496,535  *Total Assets:* £16,683,761
*Registered Office:* Suite 423, 39-41 North Road, London, N7 9DP
*Parent:* Bacchus Investments Fund S.L.U.
*Officers:* Alejandro Pedro Bulgheroni [1943] Director/Chairman & President [Argentinian/Italian]; Jose Luis Morello-Lardies [1947] Director/Vice President [Argentinian/Polish]

**Wroxeter Roman Vineyard Ltd**
*Incorporated:* 31 March 2011  *Employees:* 4
*Net Worth:* £268  *Total Assets:* £59,859
*Registered Office:* Wroxeter Roman Vineyard, The Vine House, Wroxeter, Salop, SY5 6PQ
*Shareholders:* Martin David Millington; Amanda Lynn Millington
*Officers:* Amanda Lynn Millington [1975] Director; Martin David Millington [1972] Director

**Yorkshire Heart Limited**
*Incorporated:* 17 March 2011
*Net Worth Deficit:* £163,425  *Total Assets:* £508,433
*Registered Office:* 22 Victoria Avenue, Harrogate, N Yorks, HG1 5PR
*Shareholders:* Christopher Spakouskas; Gillian Evelyn Spakouskas
*Officers:* Christopher Spakouskas [1953] Director; Gillian Evelyn Spakouskas [1954] Director

# Index of Directorships

**Abela, Albert John Martin**
Avanti Wines Ltd

**Acloque, Antoine**
Acloque Capital Limited
Viniage Wines Limited

**Ademola, Adekunle Akanji**
Fruito Beverages (Africa) Ltd

**Aje, Benson**
B & F Enterprise UK Ltd
BF Wines UK Ltd

**Alao, Lukman Abolakale**
Able G Limited

**Albu, Mihai**
Skinnybrands Ltd

**Amnegard, Goran**
Blaxsta UK Limited

**Amnegard, Lisa Alexandra**
Blaxsta UK Limited

**Andreae, Giles Edward**
The Wine Fusion Innovations Ltd

**Andres, Rowena**
Maskstice Ltd

**Antonini, Alberto**
Marmoreccia Limited

**Arbuthnot, James Norwich, Baron**
Gusbourne PLC

**Archer, Jonathan Paul Steadman**
Wild Life Botanicals Ltd

**Arora, Sunil**
Hampshire Wines Limited

**Assefaw, Alex**
Bahlina Ltd

**Atkin, Jonathan**
Noahs Estate Ltd

**Atkinson, Kieron John**
Atkinson Wines Ltd

**Avci, Ergenekon Mustafa**
Ergene Holding (UK) Ltd.

**Avis, Irene**
Sant' Elia Limited

**Avis, Jerry Philip**
Sant' Elia Limited

**Bache, Justin**
B & M Wines Ltd
Little Horse Wines Limited

**Badham, John**
Green Evolution Products Ltd

**Bagtas, Rosita**
Braidclift Ltd

**Balcombe, Dennis**
Hampshire Wines Limited

**Ball, John Richard**
Southern England Wines (UK) Ltd
Upperton Vineyards Limited

**Balmer, Kieran Patrick**
South East Wineries Limited

**Balmer, Sophie Emma Louise**
South East Wineries Limited

**Banks, Samuel N K**
AB Vaults Group Limited

**Barber, Charlotte**
Mersea Island Brewery & Vineyard Ltd

**Barber, Jacqueline**
Mersea Island Brewery & Vineyard Ltd

**Barber, Mark**
Mersea Island Brewery & Vineyard Ltd

**Barber, Roger George William**
Mersea Island Brewery & Vineyard Ltd

**Barlow, Michelle**
Sapphiremimic Ltd

**Barnes, Andrew Robert**
Sticle Vineyard Ltd

**Bartholomew, Andrew John**
Andreas Wine Trading Ltd

**Bateman, Dominic Thomas Oliver**
Maud Heath Wine Trading Ltd

**Bateman, Elizabeth**
Maud Heath Wine Trading Ltd

**Bateman, Michael William**
Maud Heath Wine Trading Ltd

**Bates, Angela Jane Primrose**
Welland Valley Vineyard Ltd

**Bates, David Stafford**
Welland Valley Vineyard Ltd

**Bath, Gareth**
Chapel Down Group PLC

**Bell, Robert**
Broadland Wineries Limited

**Bell, Thomas Neale**
Skinnybrands Ltd

**Belli, Louisa Kate Arabella**
Davenport Vineyards Limited

**Benavente, Jose Miguel**
Santa Rita Europe Limited

**Bennett, Charlotte Louise**
Gwinllan Conwy Ltd

**Bennett, Colin Stephen**
Gwinllan Conwy Ltd

**Bentham, Paul Generald**
Gusbourne PLC

**Bevilacqua, Alessandro**
Continental Wine & Food Ltd

**Bilimoria, Karan Faridoon, Lord**
General Bilimoria Wines Ltd

**Bisan-Etame Mayer, Dionisio**
Guinexport Trade and Services Ltd

**Black, Adam Richard**
The Wine Fusion Limited

**Blakey, Steven Andrew**
Hambledon Vineyard PLC
Hambledon Wineries Limited

**Bloy, Nicholas**
Coates and Seely Limited

**Boscawen, Evelyn George William**
Mereworth Wines Limited

**Brampton, Michelle Elizabeth**
Beringer Blass Wine Estates Ltd
Cellarmaster Wines Holdings (UK) Ltd
FBL Holdings Limited
James Herrick Wines Limited
The New Zealand Wine Club Ltd
Southcorp Wines Europe Limited
TWE Finance (UK) Limited
Treasury Wine Estates EMEA Ltd
Treasury Wine Estates UK Brands Ltd

**Brewer, America Rodrigues Ribeiro**
Oastbrook Estates Limited

**Brewer, Nicholas Robert**
Oastbrook Estates Limited

**Brooke, James Dominic**
Chapel Down Group PLC

**Brooksbank, Giles Patrick**
Andreas Wine Trading Ltd

**Bruce, James Henry Morys, The Honourable**
Evremond Estate Limited

**Budd, Anthony James**
Kingscote Winery Ltd

**Bulgheroni, Alejandro Pedro**
World Wine Investors UK Ltd

**Bunker, Heather**
Danbury Wine Estate Limited

**Bunker, Michael Stewart**
Danbury Wine Estate Limited

**Bunting, Thomas William**
Carter's Vineyards Ltd

**Burke, William McLean**
Rose Wine Ltd.

**Cadogan, Charles Generald John, Lord**
Evremond Estate Limited

**Cameron, Ewen Irving**
Digby Fine English Ltd
Digby Wine Ltd

**Canavan, Berendina Geertruida**
Weinhouse Limited

**Canavan, Daniel John**
Weinhouse Limited

**Carr Taylor, David Richard Thomas**
Carr Taylor Wines Limited

**Carr Taylor, Linda Rosemary**
Carr Taylor Wines Limited

**Carr, Benjamin Charles**
Podere Delle Rune Ltd

**Chance, Tim**
Strawberry Hill Vineyard Ltd

**Christie-Miller, Andrew William Michael**
Hambledon Vineyard PLC
Hambledon Wineries Limited

**Clapp, Matthew David**
Gusbourne PLC

**Clark, Matthew Nicolas**
Embev Ltd

**Clarke, George William**
Cotswold Wine Estate Ltd

**Clarke, Nicholas Antony**
Weyborne Limited

**Clavijo Barrio, Jose Ignacio**
Selectia Wine Ltd

**Cleary, Anthony Austin**
The Wine Fusion Limited

**Cleary, Veronica Anne**
The Wine Fusion Limited

**Clough, Trevor Todd**
Digby Fine English Ltd
Digby Wine Ltd

**Coates, Nicholas John**
Coates and Seely Limited

**Collyear, Emma Louise Alicia**
Winehood Ltd

**Conway, Gary Nicholas**
Skinnybrands Ltd

**Cook, Vicki Alison**
Somborne Valley Vineyard Ltd

**Cooke, Giles**
Our Fathers Wines Ltd

**Cooke, Peter Alexander**
Kingsthorne Limited

**Cooper, Nicholas John, Dr**
Albourne Winery Limited

**Corbett, Robert Henry**
Castlewood Vineyards Ltd

**Corney, Hugo**
Court Garden Limited

**Corney, Jennifer Lynn**
Court Garden Limited

**Corney, William Howard**
Court Garden Limited

**Corra, Roberta**
G.I.V. UK Ltd

**Costley, Stephen John**
Barramundi Wines Ltd

**Coulson, John Paul**
Polgoon Vineyard Ltd

**Couvreur, Marthe Georgette Andree**
Michel Couvreur (Scotch Whiskies) Ltd

**Cozens, Glynis Eileen**
Fair Services Limited

**Croft, David Michael Bruce**
Andreas Wine Trading Ltd

**Dadlani, Jairaj Jashanmal**
United Manufacturing Europe Ltd

**Daily, Keith Hugh**
The Derbyshire Winery Limited

**Dalrymple BT, Hew Richard Hamilton**
Broadland Wineries Limited

**Darby, Francesca Anna**
Winehood Ltd

**Darley, Mark Leonard**
Enborne Vineyards Limited

**Dave, Anil**
St Emilion Holdings Limited

**Davenport, William Talbot John**
Davenport Vineyards Limited

**David, Giles Matthew Oliver**
San Gregorio UK Limited

**Davidson, Neil Stuart**
Vergecosse Limited

**Davies, Iain Robert**
Henners Limited

**Davis, Adam**
The Pure Winery Limited

**De La Barra, Jaime**
Santa Rita Europe Limited

**Deakin, James**
Grape Fun Limited

**Del Rosario, Marlyn**
Bathinmaestro Ltd

**Derx, Adrian William**
Deviock Wine Co Ltd

**Deschamps, Alexandra Marie Elisabeth**
Michel Couvreur (Scotch Whiskies) Ltd

**Deschamps, Cyril**
Michel Couvreur (Scotch Whiskies) Ltd

**Deves, Alan Douglas**
Langham Wine Limited

**Devonport, Terence Viscount, Rt Hon**
Tillingham Wines Limited

**Ding, Kang**
KMSFish One Limited

**Duckett, Fiona Louise**
The Stonor Valley Winery Ltd

**Duckett, Stephen Patrick**
The Stonor Valley Winery Ltd

**Dunsmore, John Michael**
Chapel Down Group PLC

**Dyson, Brad**
The Brighton and Hove Wine Co Ltd

**Ealand, Donald Arthur**
Chiltern Valley Liqueur Producers, Brewers & Vintners

**Ealand, Duncan Fortune**
Chiltern Valley Liqueur Producers, Brewers & Vintners

**Ealand, Olivia Clare**
Chiltern Valley Liqueur Producers, Brewers & Vintners

**East, Jeffrey PM**
Alistair McCoist & Jeff East (Vintners)

**Edgar, Matthew Leonard**
Cool Brew Dept Ltd

**Edwards, Ian**
Furleigh Estate (Winery) Ltd

**Eggleston, Trevor**
Walton Brook Vineyard Limited

**Ellis, Benjamin Paul**
Chalk House Vineyard Limited

**Ellis, Samantha**
Chalk House Vineyard Limited

**Emeny, Selina Holliday**
Chapel Down Group PLC

**Englefield, Alison Jane**
South East Vineyards Association Ltd

**Engstrom, Hans Ivan**
Engstrom Group Ltd

**Evans Robson, Sarah Elizabeth**
Rothley Wine Limited

**Evans, Laura Anne**
Bibelot Wine Ltd

**Farquhar, James Thomson**
Enlightened Entrepreneur Ltd

**Fast, Jacquelyn**
Rebel Pi Limited

**Fawcett, Lucifer**
Luminati Wine Limited

**Feeney, Brendan**
Robert Roberts (NI) Limited

**Feliciano, Jamie Rose**
Audiozine Ltd

**Fistonich, George Vjeceslav, Sir**
Villa Maria New Zealand Wineries (UK)

**Fistonich, Karen Theresa**
Villa Maria New Zealand Wineries (UK)

**Fleetwood, James**
Forgeron Dubois Limited

**Foley, Conor**
Swift Half Collective Ltd

**Foroshani, Keyvan**
K1 Beer PLC

**Fossati, Maria Elena**
G.I.V. UK Ltd

**Fowke, Elaine Frances**
Green Ridge Wines Ltd

**Fowke, Martin Hoult**
The Global Winery Limited
Three Choirs Vineyards Limited

**Fox, Gerard Ian**
Mayfield Vineyards Ltd
Sussex Vineyards Limited

**Fox, Jonica Mary Mandeville**
Mayfield Vineyards Ltd

**Frantzen, Jean Arnaud**
Michel Couvreur (Scotch Whiskies) Ltd

**French, Stephanie**
Green Evolution Production Ltd

**Gadingan, Giselle**
Skyblossom Ltd

**Garcia-Benito, Balbina Patricia**
Bsixtwelve Limited

**Gauntlett, Conrad Martin**
Rosemary Vineyard Ltd.

**Gayler, Graham Anthony**
Ridgeview Estate Winery Ltd

**Gibbons, Andrew William**
Amwell Springs Brewery Co Ltd

**Gibbons, David Ernest**
Amwell Springs Brewery Co Ltd

**Gibbons, Michael David**
Amwell Springs Brewery Co Ltd

**Gidley, Paul Anthony**
The Pure Winery Limited

**Gile, Russiene**
Mosrowes Ltd

**Gladwin, Bridget**
Nutbourne Vineyards Limited

**Gladwin, Peter Alexis**
Nutbourne Vineyards Limited

**Gleave, David Charles**
La Remonta Limited

**Gobbi, Marco**
G.I.V. UK Ltd

**Gorrichon, Pierrick**
Somm in the Must Ltd

**Goss-Custard, Daniel James**
Stanlake Park Co Ltd

**Gowan, Catriona Mary**
Torview Wines Limited

**Gowan, Timothy**
Torview Wines Limited

**Granger, Antony**
Green Evolution Products Ltd

**Green, Bruce Stuart**
Hattingley Valley Wines Ltd

**Greenwood, James Lawrence, Dr**
Barramundi Wines Ltd

**Grey, James**
Rockfield Wines Limited

**Griffiths, Ceri**
Walton Brook Vineyard Limited

**Griffiths, David**
The Global Winery Limited

**Guibert, Christelle Anita**
Vine Revival UK Limited

**Hafstad, Einar Finn**
Medland Manor Vineyard Ltd.

**Hall, Christine Janet**
Breaky Bottom Ltd

**Hall, Mark John**
Winebar Pouch Co Ltd

**Hall, Nicholas Morton**
Herbert Hall Wines Limited

**Hall, Peter Anthony Inglis**
Breaky Bottom Ltd

**Ham, Daniel**
Langham Wine Limited

**Ham, Daniel Nicholas**
Press Shed Wines Limited

**Ham, Nicola Anne, Dr**
Press Shed Wines Limited

**Hammond, Thomas James**
Amwell Springs Brewery Co Ltd

**Hansford, Rebecca Ruth**
Furleigh Estate (Winery) Ltd

**Hardingham, Barbara Eileen**
Ludlow Vineyard Limited

**Hardingham, Michael John**
Ludlow Vineyard Limited

**Hariyani, Aashima**
Globus Wines (UK) Ltd

**Harris, Philip Lewis**
Davenport Vineyards Limited

**Harvey, Mark Simon**
Chapel Down Group PLC

**Hawkins, Colin Charles**
D'Urberville Vineyard Limited

**Heasman, Gunvor Birgitta**
Black Dog Hill Estates Ltd

**Heasman, Raymond George**
Black Dog Hill Estates Ltd

**Heerema, Eric Niels**
Nyetimber (International Operations)
Nyetimber Limited

**Helliwell, Christine Sarah, Dr**
Heron Ventures Ltd

**Helliwell, Peter John**
Heron Ventures Ltd

**Hepworth-Bond, Thomas Huw**
Enlightened Entrepreneur Ltd

**Hewson, Thomas David**
Crundale Wines Limited

**Hickey, John Patrick**
Binfield Vineyard Limited

**Hipwell, Adrian Paul**
Flint & Vine Limited

**Hobson, Linda**
Somerby Vineyards Limited

**Hobson, William**
Somerby Vineyards Limited

**Hodge, Craig**
Amor Food and Beverages Holdings Ltd

**Holland, Charles Edward**
Gusbourne PLC

**Hope, Andrew**
Bluebell Vineyard Estates Ltd

**Hope, John Michael**
The Wine Fusion Innovations Ltd

**Howard, Catherine Linda**
Giffords Hall Vineyard Limited

**Howard, Guy Halsall**
Giffords Hall Vineyard Limited

**Hu, Weiqing**
Daavan Two Limited

**Hughes D'Aeth, Paul Andrew**
Evremond Vineyards Limited

**Hulme, Flora Elsie**
Fleur Fields Limited

**Hulme, William Allen**
Fleur Fields Limited

**Humphries, Jason John, Dr**
Digby Fine English Ltd
Digby Wine Ltd

**Hunter, Peter Michael John**
Swift Half Collective Ltd

**Hurst, Anne-Marie**
Drinktonics Limited
The Flower Miners Limited

**Hutchison, Gregory Iain**
Barramundi Wines Ltd

**Jacobsohn, Douglas**
Busi-Jacobsohn Wine Estate Ltd

**James, Janice**
Silverton Wines Ltd

**Jansen, Johan Willem Maarten**
The Pure Winery Limited

**Jarrett, Leslie**
Shawsgate Limited

**Jolly, Prem**
Premia Wines Ltd.

**Jones, Julie**
Pharos AC Ltd.

**Jordan, Ivan James**
Silverton Wines Ltd

**Joynt, David Andrew**
Acloque Capital Limited
Viniage Wines Limited

**Kato, Archard Lwihula**
Alko Vintages UK Ltd

**Kearney, Seamus**
Robert Roberts (NI) Limited

**Kellett, Ian James**
Hambledon Vineyard PLC
Hambledon Wineries Limited

**Kelly, John Eric**
Barramundi Wines Ltd

**Kendall, Niamh**
Kidmore Vineyard Ltd

**Kendall, Stephen**
Kidmore Vineyard Ltd

**Keukenmeester, Nicholas John**
Heartland Wines Europe Limited

**Khachidze, Bachana**
Bach & Co Solution Limited

**Khan, Victoria**
Tewaina Ltd

**Kimber, Lawrence George**
Dinton Wines Limited

**King, John Watson**
Vergecosse Limited

**Klat, George Michel**
Wolf Oak Limited

**Kolflaath, Gerhard**
Arctic Wine Limited
Vesteraalen Vinproduksjon Ltd

**Krajewski, Martin John**
St Emilion Holdings Limited

**Kuester, Dieter Heinz Friedrich**
T & P Weinbau

**Kutty, Zack**
Realsa Wines Import & Export Ltd

**Laithwaite, Henry John Hugh**
Harrow & Hope Limited

**Laithwaite, Kaye Louise**
Harrow & Hope Limited

**Lane, Marie Elise**
Laneberg Wine Ltd

**Langham, John Christopher**
Langham Wine Limited

**Langham, Justin Morley**
Langham Wine Limited

**Langham, Lynn Patricia**
A'Beckett's Vineyard Limited

**Langham, Paul Brook**
A'Beckett's Vineyard Limited

**Lansley, Jonathon Mark**
Broadland Wineries Limited

**Lanson, Jean Victor**
Victor Lanson Limited
Lanson UK Limited

**Lavados, Andres**
Santa Rita Europe Limited

**Lavalle, Dianne Jerica**
Uponcellar Ltd

**Lawrence, Tara**
Little Horse Wines Limited

**Le Grice, Marcus Andrew**
St Emilion Holdings Limited

**Le Sueur, Damien Bruno Paul Marie**
Evremond Estate Limited

**Lebond, David Christopher**
Andreas Wine Trading Ltd

**Lee, Joanne Elizabeth**
Eco Vino Limited

**Lennard, Tomas Woody**
Montgomery Vineyard Limited

**Lewis, Barry**
Amber Valley Wines Ltd

**Lindo, Robert Walter**
Camel Valley Limited

**Lindo, Samuel Robert**
Camel Valley Limited

**Linter, Samantha Martha**
Bolney Vineyards Ltd
Bolney Wine Estate Ltd

**Lobo, Rudolf John Gabriel**
Kingscote Investments Limited
South East Wineries Limited

**Lorinkov, Alexander**
Karmely Limited

**Ludbrook, Hamish William**
Oui Vino Limited

**Mann, Anthony**
Port O' Bristol Ltd

**Marquez, Francisca Isabel**
Selectia Wine Ltd

**Marriot, Patrick Charles Stewart**
Cotswold Wine Estate Ltd

**Martorana, Giuseppe**
Gavioli Ltd

**Mastrapasqua, Sabino Antonio**
Mastropasqua & Brothers Ltd.

**Matsumoto, Kenya**
B & M Wines Ltd

**Maxwell, Gareth Howard**
Hattingley Valley Wines Ltd

**McAlindon, Kevin Peter**
Duncairn Wines Limited

**McAlindon, Neal Edward**
Duncairn Wines Limited

**McCay, Danny**
Swift Half Collective Ltd

**McCoist, Alistair Murdoch**
Alistair McCoist & Jeff East (Vintners)

**McCredie, Duncan**
Magnus Wines Ltd

**McEwan, Feona Mary**
Dropmore Vineyard Ltd

**McGirr, Grahame**
Gavioli Ltd

**McGrath, Patrick William**
Evremond Estate Limited

**McKeon, Adrian Francis**
Accolade Wines Limited

**McMackin, James Generald**
Alcohol Beverages Co Ltd

**McTernan Mann, Lela**
Port O' Bristol Ltd

**Mehta, Ankit**
Universal Robo Innovations Ltd

**Millington, Amanda Lynn**
Wroxeter Roman Vineyard Ltd

**Millington, Martin David**
Wroxeter Roman Vineyard Ltd

**Mitchell, Rosanna Laura**
Sibling Winery Limited

**Monge, Christen Andrew**
Kingscote Winery Ltd

**Monteiro, Antonio**
Amont Products Limited

**Moreina Valente, Elaine**
Amont Products Limited

**Morello-Lardies, Jose Luis**
World Wine Investors UK Ltd

**Moreno Garcia-Campero, Mario Jose**
Pharos AC Ltd.

**Moriarty, Michael Joseph**
Henners Limited

**Morley, Katharine Helena**
Three Choirs Vineyards Limited

**Morris, Mark**
Celebrated Wines Limited

**Nattrass, Mark Stephen, Dr**
Tremayne Food and Drink Ltd

**Ng, Belinda Boon-Leen**
Bluebell Vineyard Estates Ltd

**Ng, Tock Sinn**
Bluebell Vineyard Estates Ltd

**Nielsen, Robert Emil**
Brightday Enterprises Limited

**Nightingale, Alison Jane**
Albourne Winery Limited

**Noble, Laurence David**
De Noble Vines Limited

**Nolan, Anja Gunvor Heasman**
Black Dog Hill Estates Ltd

**Nolan, James Peter**
Black Dog Hill Estates Ltd

**Oenga, Elkanah Ondieki**
Alko Vintages UK Ltd

**Pankhurst, Chloe**
River Valley Vineyards Limited

**Pankhurst, Stuart**
River Valley Vineyards Limited

**Parulan, Ethel Joy**
Nuclearbest Ltd

**Pascual, Anthony**
Bigmite Ltd

**Paul, Michael Anthony Keyes**
Gusbourne PLC

**Pavitt, Darren Rudkin**
Amwell Springs Brewery Co Ltd

**Penny, Kate Huntsman**
Conradie-Penhill Wines UK Ltd.

**Philips, Richard Haydon**
Vergecosse Limited

**Picard, Michel Bernard**
Spirits Development & Management Company (SDMC)

**Piech, Florian**
Danebury Vineyards Limited

**Pierlot, Clement Albert**
Pinglestone Estate Limited

**Pierron, Nicolas**
Somm in the Must Ltd

**Pierson, Didier**
Piersons Spirit of Wine Consulting Ltd

**Pike, Adrian**
Westwell Wine Estates Ltd

**Pinto, Helena**
Wines of Douro Limited

**Pippard, Alice Rose**
Beacon Down Vineyard Ltd

**Pippard, Paul Sutton**
Beacon Down Vineyard Ltd

**Pollard, Jonathan David**
Gusbourne PLC

**Porter, Simon**
Itasca Wines Limited

**Porton, Andrew George**
The Wine Fusion Innovations Ltd
The Wine Fusion Limited

**Prasad, Umesh**
Vitosha Wine Ltd

**Pratt, Rodney Vince**
Bolney Vineyards Ltd
Bolney Wine Estate Ltd

**Prowse, Nichola Clare**
Dorchester Vineyard Limited

**Prowse, Nicholas**
Dorchester Vineyard Limited

**Punzalan, Julius Eldrid**
Aeropica Ltd

**Pye, Jasper Orlando**
Cotswold Wine Estate Ltd

**Racine, Cedric**
Sticle Vineyard Ltd

**Racine, Christiane**
Sticle Vineyard Ltd

**Racine, Justin**
Sticle Vineyard Ltd

**Racine, Lea**
Sticle Vineyard Ltd

**Racine, Vincent**
Sticle Vineyard Ltd

**Ramirez, Hernando**
Luxbev Limited

**Reeves, Robert Anthony**
Vergecosse Limited

**Renwick, Richard John**
Beringer Blass Wine Estates Ltd
Cellarmaster Wines Holdings (UK) Ltd
FBL Holdings Limited
James Herrick Wines Limited
The New Zealand Wine Club Ltd
Southcorp Wines Europe Limited
TWE Finance (UK) Limited
Treasury Wine Estates EMEA Ltd
Treasury Wine Estates UK Brands Ltd

**Rice, Emma Mary**
Hattingley Valley Wines Ltd

**Richards, Stephen**
San Gregorio UK Limited

**Rippon, Matthew Bennett**
Creoda's Hill Ltd

**Roberson, Clifford John**
London Cru Ltd

**Roberts, Christine Pamela**
Ridgeview Estate Winery Ltd
Ridgeview Winery Contracts Ltd

**Roberts, Daniel**
Lakemercy Ltd

**Roberts, Michael William**
Dedham Vale Vineyard Limited

**Roberts, Simon Matthew**
Ridgeview Estate Winery Ltd

**Roberts, Tamara**
Ridgeview Estate Winery Ltd

**Roberts, Tamara Jane**
Ridgeview Winery Contracts Ltd

**Robinson, Alexander Benjamin Melland**
Hattingley Valley Wines Ltd

**Robinson, Ian Booth**
Lindisfarne Limited

**Robinson, Ian George**
Gusbourne Estate Limited
Gusbourne PLC

**Robinson, Nicola Jane**
Hattingley Valley Wines Ltd

**Robinson, Pamela Joy**
Creative Wine Making Limited

**Robinson, Peter William**
Creative Wine Making Limited

**Robinson, Samuel David**
Creative Wine Making Limited

**Robinson, William Martin**
Hambledon Vineyard PLC
Hambledon Wineries Limited

**Robinson, William Simon Melland**
Hattingley Valley Wines Ltd

**Robson, Peter**
Casa Vizzini Ltd

**Robson, Peter Joseph**
Devine Distillates Group (Manufacturing)

**Rowley, Lesley Anne**
Dryhill Wine Ltd

**Rowley, Nigel Graham**
Dryhill Wine Ltd

**Rudd, Timothy Nigel**
Rudd Farms Limited

**Ruigrok, Charles**
Witham Wines Limited

**Ruigrok, Gemma**
Witham Wines Limited

**Rushmere, Colin Bryan**
The Pure Winery Limited

**Sacha, Andrew Charles**
The Vineyard Dynamics Co. Ltd

**Sacha, James George**
The Vineyard Dynamics Co. Ltd

**Saflor, Anthony**
Nimblusher Ltd

**Sandbach, Henry Alistair Samuel**
Enjoy Wine Ltd

**Sargent, Ann**
Laurel Vines, Vineyard & Winery Ltd

**Sargent, Ian Leslie**
Laurel Vines, Vineyard & Winery Ltd

**Satchwell, Mark Anthony**
The Wine Fusion Limited

**Saunders, Michael Potter**
Coates and Seely Limited

**Sauvao, Eddie**
Bath Sparkling Wine Co Ltd

**Sauvao, Emily**
Bath Sparkling Wine Co Ltd

**Scarcella, Amy Louisa**
Lines Brew Co Ltd

**Scarlett, John Philip Henri**
Westwell Wine Estates Ltd

**Schonlaub, Thomas**
Schoenlaub Limited

**Seely, Christian James Russell**
Coates and Seely Limited

**Sequeira, Gaylord Carlos Aurelien**
Pinglestone Estate Limited

**Sharman, Mark Richard William**
Sharpham Partnership Limited
Sharpham Wine Limited

**Sharples, Leon Keith, Dr**
Leskaroon Falls Wine Estate Ltd

**Shaw, Brian**
Too Far North Wine Co Ltd

**Shaw, Thomas Richard Rogers**
Three Choirs Vineyards Limited

**Shiner, Fiona Jane**
Woodchester Valley Winery Ltd

**Shinwell, John David**
Continental Wine & Food Ltd

**Shouler, Henry Bonner**
Three Choirs Vineyards Limited

**Simpson, Charles William**
Simpsons Wine Estate Limited
Simpsons Wine Imports Limited

**Simpson, Ruth Elizabeth**
Simpsons Wine Estate Limited
Simpsons Wine Imports Limited

**Smith, Andrew Peter**
Accolade Wines Limited

**Smith, Christopher Luke**
The Wine Fusion Innovations Ltd

**Smith, Daniel Keith**
Sibling Winery Limited

**Smith, Guy Christopher**
Bibelot Wine Ltd

**Smith, Ian Terence**
Kingwood Estate Limited

**Smith, John Warwick**
Urban Initiatives Limited

**Smith, Michael Norman**
Southern England Wines (UK) Ltd
Upperton Vineyards Limited

**Smith, Patrick James**
Sibling Winery Limited

**Smith, Patrick Matthew**
The Global Winery Limited

**Smith, Paul Richard**
Kingscote Investments Limited
South East Wineries Limited

**Smith, Timothy James**
Forgeron Dubois Limited

**Spakouskas, Christopher**
Yorkshire Heart Limited

**Spakouskas, Gillian Evelyn**
Yorkshire Heart Limited

**Srao, Vijay Singh**
Boars Hill Farm Limited

**Stanbridge, Paul John**
Stangro Limited

**Stanbridge, Raymond John, Dr**
Stangro Limited

**Stanbridge, Sidney John**
Stangro Limited

**Steel, James Ian**
Casa Divertente Limited

**Steel, Janette Anne**
Casa Divertente Limited

**Steevenson, Liam James**
Global Wine Solutions Limited

**Stephen, Daniel**
Great Canney Vineyards Limited

**Stephen, Tom**
Great Canney Vineyards Limited

**Stephenson, Keith Caville**
Lindisfarne Limited

**Stevens, Andrew Charles**
Ghenos Vineyard Estates Ltd

**Stevens, Dora**
Ghenos Vineyard Estates Ltd

**Strachey, Henry**
Penselwood Partnership Ltd

**Strachey, Susan**
Penselwood Partnership Ltd

**Stroumpoulis, Antonios**
Qualpro Greece Ltd.

**Studzinski, Kristina Mary**
Off The Line Limited

**Sugden, Henry Francis Austin**
Defined Wine Ltd

**Sugrue, Dermot**
Sugrue Pierre Limited

**Symington, John Andrew Douglas**
Silva and Cosens Limited

**Symington, Paul Douglas**
Silva and Cosens Limited

**Symington, Rupert Alexander Douglas**
Silva and Cosens Limited

**Tainton, Jonathon David Charles**
Grape Fun Limited

**Tait, Ronald Thomas**
Lindisfarne Limited

**Taittinger, Clovis**
Evremond Estate Limited

**Taittinger, Pierre-Emmanuel**
Evremond Estate Limited

**Tarli, Fiammetta**
Fiamma & Ivo Limited

**Tay, Barry Boon Shek**
Bluebell Vineyard Estates Ltd
Plummerden Estates Limited
Plummerden Lane Vineyards Ltd

**Tay, Joyce Guat Kheng**
Bluebell Vineyard Estates Ltd
Plummerden Estates Limited
Plummerden Lane Vineyards Ltd

**Taylor, Alexander David Nicholas**
Taylor Family Wines Ltd.

**Taylor, Naomi Alexandra**
Taylor Family Wines Ltd.

**Taylor, Peter John**
Continental Wine & Food Ltd

**Taylor, Rosemary Anne**
Westwell Wine Estates Ltd

**Thackeray, Ben**
Ben Flower Limited

**Thomas, Helen Maureen**
The Global Winery Limited

**Thomas, Maxwell Hugh**
Poulton Hill Estate Limited

**Thompson, Frazer Douglas**
Chapel Down Group PLC
English Wines PLC

**Thompson, Nathan Edward**
The Clandestine Distillery Ltd

**Thompson, Sarah**
The Boutique Cellar Limited

**Tilbrook, Grantley Bill**
Heartland Wines Europe Limited

**Tinston, Liam**
Tinston Wines & Ciders Limited

**Toseafa, Caroline**
Caxdon Premier Limited

**Toseafa, Donald**
Caxdon Premier Limited

**Travis, Jane**
Atkinson Wines Ltd

**Trimming, Paul**
Penselwood Partnership Ltd

**Trinchero, Louis**
Sutter Home Winery Limited

**Trinchero, Roger John**
Sutter Home Winery Limited

**Tukker, Arie**
Ridgeview Estate Winery Ltd

**Turner, Ashley Ryck**
Sloegasm Limited

**Tynan, Ann-Marie**
Off The Line Limited

**Vasudevan, Shinoj**
Realsa Wines Import & Export Ltd

**Verrillo, Lynsey Abernethy**
The Verrillo Partnership Ltd

**Verrillo, Sergio Milan**
The Verrillo Partnership Ltd

**Vickers, Clive Martin Charles**
Gowine Limited

**Vranken, Paul-Francois Edouard Joseph**
Pinglestone Estate Limited

**Wagstaff, Hilary Mary**
Greyfriars Vineyard Limited

**Wagstaff, Michael John**
Greyfriars Vineyard Limited

**Wainvenhaus, Charlotte**
Danebury Vineyards Limited

**Walgate, Ben**
UK Wine Services Limited

**Walgate, Benjamin James**
Tillingham Wines Limited

**Walker, Daniel**
Oeno Group Ltd

**Walker, Malcolm Thomas**
Itasca Wines Limited

**Walsh, John Michael**
Strawberry Bank Liqueurs Ltd

**Walwyn-James, Christopher Darryl**
Lindisfarne Limited

**Wang, Hongxiao**
Ross Earl Wine Co., Ltd.

**Weeber, Andrew Carl Vincent**
Gusbourne Estate Limited
Gusbourne PLC

**Wenman, Nicholas Edward**
South East Vineyards Association Ltd

**West, Bernard John, Dr**
Harmony Vineyard Ltd.

**West, Fiona**
Harmony Vineyard Ltd.

**West, Jo-Ann**
Polmassick Vineyard Limited

**West, Nicholas William**
Polmassick Vineyard Limited

**White, Juliet Anne**
Exe Valley Wines Limited

**Whiteley, Dennis**
Henners Limited

**Williams, Nigel Grenville, Dr**
Highbrook Wine Estate Limited

**Williams, Sarah Louise**
Vinus Wine Ltd

**Williams, Veronica Mary**
Highbrook Wine Estate Limited

**Wilson, Janice**
Dedham Vale Vineyard Limited

**Witchell, Benjamin James**
Flint & Vine Limited

**Witchell, Hannah Mary**
Flint & Vine Limited

**Wolstenholme, Jacqueline**
Somborne Valley Vineyard Ltd

**Wolstenholme, Nigel Timothy**
Somborne Valley Vineyard Ltd

**Wood, Anthony Graham**
Accolade Wines Limited

**Wood, David Derek**
Bolney Wine Estate Ltd

**Woodhead, Simon Martin**
Stopham Vineyard Ltd

**Woodhouse, Richard Alexander Bruce**
Chapel Down Group Ltd
Chapel Down Group PLC
English Wines PLC

**Wray, Nigel William**
Chapel Down Group PLC

**Wren, Simon Timothy**
Westwell Wine Estates Ltd

**Yakich, Fabian George**
Villa Maria New Zealand Wineries (UK)

**Zhang, Weicheng**
Digby Fine English Ltd
Digby Wine Ltd

# Standard Industrial Classification
*excluding*
*Manufacture of wine from grape*

**01110 Growing of cereals (except rice), leguminous crops and oil seeds**
Boars Hill Farm Limited

**01130 Growing of vegetables and melons, roots and tubers**
Boars Hill Farm Limited

**01210 Growing of grapes** [20]
Beacon Down Vineyard Ltd
Boars Hill Farm Limited
Bsixtwelve Limited
Crundale Wines Limited
Harmony Vineyard Ltd.
Oastbrook Estates Limited
Off The Line Limited
Pinglestone Estate Limited
Polmassick Vineyard Limited
Ridgeview Estate Winery Ltd
Sant' Elia Limited
Southern England Wines (UK) Ltd
Stanlake Park Co Ltd
Sticle Vineyard Ltd
Tewaina Ltd
UK Wine Services Limited
Upperton Vineyards Limited
Weyborne Limited
Wolf Oak Limited
Wroxeter Roman Vineyard Ltd

**01260 Growing of oleaginous fruits**
Sant' Elia Limited

**01270 Growing of beverage crops**
Sibling Winery Limited

**01500 Mixed farming**
Sharpham Partnership Limited

**10410 Manufacture of oils and fats**
Sant' Elia Limited

**10511 Liquid milk and cream production**
Sharpham Partnership Limited

**10720 Manufacture of rusks and biscuits; manufacture of preserved pastry goods and cakes**
Amor Food and Beverages Holdings Ltd

**10840 Manufacture of condiments and seasonings**
Tremayne Food and Drink Ltd

**11010 Distilling, rectifying and blending of spirits** [14]
Alko Vintages UK Ltd
Boutique Cellar Limited
Clandestine Distillery Limited
Cool Brew Dept Ltd
Michel Couvreur (Scotch Whiskies)
Devine Distillates Group (Manufacturing)
K1 Beer PLC
Ludlow Vineyard Limited
Luxbev Limited
Mastropasqua & Brothers Ltd.
Skinnybrands Ltd
Spirits Development & Management Company (SDMC)
Swift Half Collective Ltd
Universal Robo Innovations Ltd

**11030 Manufacture of cider and other fruit wines** [23]
AB Vaults Group Limited
Alcohol Beverages Co Ltd
BF Wines UK Ltd
Boutique Cellar Limited
Broadland Wineries Limited
Caxdon Premier Limited
Clandestine Distillery Limited
Cool Brew Dept Ltd
Creoda's Hill Ltd
Embev Ltd
Flower Miners Limited
Kingscote Winery Ltd
Lines Brew Co Ltd
Ludlow Vineyard Limited
Luminati Wine Limited
Medland Manor Vineyard Ltd.
Noahs Estate Ltd
Polgoon Vineyard Ltd
Sharpham Wine Limited
Sibling Winery Limited
Tinston Wines & Ciders Limited
Tremayne Food and Drink Ltd
Wild Life Botanicals Ltd

**11040 Manufacture of other non-distilled fermented beverages**
Amwell Springs Brewery Co Ltd
Cool Brew Dept Ltd
Fruito Beverages (Africa) Ltd
Mastropasqua & Brothers Ltd.
Tremayne Food and Drink Ltd
Universal Robo Innovations Ltd

**11050 Manufacture of beer** [12]
Alcohol Beverages Co Ltd
Amwell Springs Brewery Co Ltd
Boutique Cellar Limited
Clandestine Distillery Limited
K1 Beer PLC
Luxbev Limited
Mersea Island Brewery & Vineyard Ltd
Skinnybrands Ltd
Swift Half Collective Ltd
Universal Robo Innovations Ltd
Vitosha Wine Ltd
Yorkshire Heart Limited

**11060 Manufacture of malt**
AB Vaults Group Limited
Devine Distillates Group (Manufacturing)
Fruito Beverages (Africa) Ltd

**11070 Manufacture of soft drinks; production of mineral waters and other bottled waters**
AB Vaults Group Limited
Alko Vintages UK Ltd
Amor Food and Beverages Holdings Ltd
Fruito Beverages (Africa) Ltd
Luxbev Limited
Vitosha Wine Ltd
Wild Life Botanicals Ltd

**13300 Finishing of textiles**
Ergene Holding (UK) Ltd.

**15120 Manufacture of luggage, handbags and the like, saddlery and harness**
Ergene Holding (UK) Ltd.

**18201 Reproduction of sound recording**
Fiamma & Ivo Limited

**32990 Other manufacturing n.e.c.**
Eco Vino Limited

**41100 Development of building projects**
Engstrom Group Ltd
K1 Beer PLC

**46170 Agents involved in the sale of food, beverages and tobacco**
Cellarmaster Wines Holdings (UK) Ltd
Direct Wine Factory Ltd

**46342 Wholesale of wine, beer, spirits and other alcoholic beverages** [46]
Alko Vintages UK Ltd
Amwell Springs Brewery Co Ltd
B & F Enterprise UK Ltd
BF Wines UK Ltd
Bach & Co Solution Limited
Brighton and Hove Wine Co Ltd
Michel Couvreur (Scotch Whiskies)
Crundale Wines Limited
D'Urberville Vineyard Limited
Davenport Vineyards Limited
Digby Fine English Ltd
Digby Wine Ltd
Direct Wine Factory Ltd
Drinktonics Limited
Duncairn Wines Limited
Flower Miners Limited
General Bilimoria Wines Ltd
Globus Wines (UK) Ltd
Guinexport Trade and Services Ltd
Harrow & Hope Limited
Itasca Wines Limited
Laneberg Wine Ltd
Lindisfarne Limited
Little Horse Wines Limited
Magnus Wines Ltd
Alistair McCoist & Jeff East (Vintners)
Noahs Estate Ltd
Oui Vino Limited
Pinglestone Estate Limited
Realsa Wines Import & Export Ltd
Rebel Pi Limited
Ross Earl Wine Co., Ltd.
Schoenlaub Limited
Selectia Wine Ltd
Sharpham Wine Limited
Simpsons Wine Imports Limited
Somborne Valley Vineyard Ltd
Somm in the Must Ltd
Southern England Wines (UK) Ltd
Spirits Development & Management Company (SDMC)
Tewaina Ltd
Verrillo Partnership Limited
Vitosha Wine Ltd
Wild Life Botanicals Ltd
Wine Fusion Limited
Winehood Ltd

# The UK Wine Industry

**46390 Non-specialised wholesale of food, beverages and tobacco**
Lindisfarne Limited

**47250 Retail sale of beverages in specialised stores**
Davenport Vineyards Limited
Direct Wine Factory Ltd
Drinktonics Limited
Duncairn Wines Limited
Laneberg Wine Ltd
Alistair McCoist & Jeff East (Vintners)
Sharpham Wine Limited
Stanlake Park Co Ltd

**47290 Other retail sale of food in specialised stores**
Guinexport Trade and Services Ltd

**47520 Retail sale of hardware, paints and glass in specialised stores**
Lindisfarne Limited

**55300 Recreational vehicle parks, trailer parks and camping grounds**
Heron Ventures Ltd

**56101 Licenced restaurants**
Continental Wine & Food Ltd
Ghenos Vineyard Estates Ltd
Tillingham Wines Limited

**56290 Other food services**
Enjoy Wine Ltd

**64209 Activities of other holding companies n.e.c.**
Gusbourne PLC

**64303 Activities of venture and development capital companies**
Gavioli Ltd

**68209 Other letting and operating of own or leased real estate**
Kingscote Investments Limited
South East Wineries Limited
Tewaina Ltd

**70100 Activities of head offices**
General Bilimoria Wines Ltd

**70221 Financial management**
Engstrom Group Ltd

**70229 Management consultancy activities other than financial management**
UK Wine Services Limited
Vinus Wine Ltd

**74909 Other professional, scientific and technical activities n.e.c.**
Eco Vino Limited
Pharos AC Ltd.

**80200 Security systems service activities**
B & F Enterprise UK Ltd

**80300 Investigation activities**
B & F Enterprise UK Ltd

**81300 Landscape service activities**
Michel Couvreur (Scotch Whiskies)
Maud Heath Wine Trading Ltd

**82990 Other business support service activities n.e.c.**
Carr Taylor Wines Limited
Strawberry Bank Liqueurs Ltd

**85590 Other education n.e.c.**
Heron Ventures Ltd

**96090 Other service activities n.e.c.**
Schoenlaub Limited

**98000 Residents property management**
Engstrom Group Ltd

**99999 Dormant company**
Off The Line Limited

*This page is intentionally left blank*

Printed in 8pt Nimbus Sans L

Designed by URW++ Design and Development GmbH

Dellam Publishing Limited

2 Heath Drive, Sutton, Surrey, SM2 5RP

Fax: 020 8770 7478     email: enquiries@dellam.com

SAN: 0177881     EAN/GLN: 5030670177882

www.ingramcontent.com/pod-product-compliance
Lightning Source LLC
Chambersburg PA
CBHW081128080526
44587CB00021B/3791